never a time
to trust

The Carnivore of Many Names:

Felis Concolor is the Latin name.

Cougar is Western Canadian.

Panther and Painter were names used by the settlers of Eastern Canada and the United States.

Both Mountain Lion and Catamount were names used in the high country of the West.

Puma is a much-used name in the mountains of South America and sometimes here.

Indian Devil, wildcat and ghost cat are used in local areas of North America.

Varmint is the name my South Carolina born dad used but the British Columbia Game Department referred to them as vermin during earlier years.

never a time to trust

A story of
British Columbia,
her pioneers, predators and problems

For: Gale + Rod Parisien
joe garner July 5-1986

Best Wishes — Joe Garner

Cinnabar Press

Nanaimo, British Columbia
1984

First printing November 1984
Second printing December 1984
Second edition, revised, February 1985
Second printing October 1985

Available at most book outlets at $9.95
or order direct from:

Cinnabar Press
P.O. Box 392
Nanaimo, B.C., Canada V9R 5L3

Cover painting and illustrations by Pat Wright.

Published by
CINNABAR PRESS
P.O. Box 392
Nanaimo, B.C., Canada V9R 5L3

Designed and printed in Canada by
MORRISS PRINTING COMPANY LTD.
Victoria, British Columbia

To the Memory of Jimmy Dewar,
Albert Holman,
and my brother Tom,
who shared with me their knowledge
of the outdoors.

Contents

Maps on pages 14, 15 and 129
Illustrations follow pages 64, 96 and 168

Preface

Never A Time To Trust is written about the outdoors. The book recalls the pioneers who started the first game regulations.

Covered here is a series of events involving Cougar (*Felis Concolor*), the largest native cat in North America. Their greatest densities are found on Vancouver Island. They are also found on practically every island along the mainland coast from the State of Washington to Bella Coola. The book is written to show the changes and conditions leading up to the present day game policies.

Born in 1909, I remember times when there was more virgin timber, more birds and wildlife and about one third as many hunters.

With the advent of thousands of miles of logging roads, four-wheel drive vehicles, imported hounds, two-way radios and aircraft, it is imperative adjustments be made to protect our wildlife.

Although the cougar is the most secretive, it is also the most vulnerable of all our big game species when hunted with hounds.

My first encounter with a cougar occurred before my ninth birthday. It's a miracle I escaped to tell about it. The incident left me with a great distrust of the big cats.

J. G.

Acknowledgements

I would like to extend my sincere thanks to the following people:

Ruby King for her encouragement, assistance and design.

Barry Broadfoot for the foreword and editing.

Pat Wright for the front cover and illustrations.

Bob Akerman and his family for pictures and other reliable material.

All of the Albert Holman family for interviews and pictures.

Jack and Dan Lay for information and interviews.

Frank Greenfield for pictures and background material.

Tom MacDonald for West Coast information and numerous other people who gave willingly of their time.

Pat Meier for typing the manuscript.

Maralyn Horsdal for editorial advice.

Dick Morriss and his friendly staff who transformed the manuscript and pictures into a quality book.

Joe Garner

Foreword

I met Joe Garner in 1981, autumn, when his first book, *Never Fly Over An Eagle's Nest*, was published and he was to speak to the Nanaimo Rotary Club luncheon.

While we chatted over a drink before lunch he asked, "God, what will I talk to them about?" and I answered, "Joe, I'm a guest so I don't know these guys but I'll bet none of them ever sat down and wrote a book about his life and you've done it. Get up there and tell them why you did it and what it's about," and I tapped him on the shoulder and said, "Ride 'em, Cowboy!"

Now here's a man, a pioneer British Columbian in every sense, then 72 years old, born in a log cabin with a dirt floor, shot his first buck at eight, saved his own life by outrunning and outjumping a tom cougar at nine, worked in logging, owned logging and construction firms, pioneered helicopter logging which may be the saviour of the forest industry some day, fought high seas and hard tides, made a major contribution to the war effort, a bush pilot with his own airline, a

11

hunter par excellence, a tough guy, a good fellow, and he's standing up there in front of men he's known for many a year, and he is scared. You know, shaking.

He looked at his fellow Rotarians and said, "Well, I really don't know what to say," and I called out, "Ride 'em, Cowboy!" Joe took off for more than his allotted time and he just let 'er rip! When he finished he waved his book and said, "Well, fellows, here it is, I done it," and the banquet room burst into hard and steady applause and there was no mistaking it, every man-Jack of them was thinking, 'Joe did it and I wish I had.'

Never Fly Over An Eagle's Nest went on to be a best seller and through Joe's efforts and those of Ruby King, hundreds of people right through to Halifax read it because they sold books like authors of olden days did. They piled a ton of books into Joe's big van and got out where the people were and went on radio, TV and in the press and he'd say, "Here's my book about my life and I like it and I hope you like it," and encouraged by his confident but quiet way of speaking, they bought it and they liked it.

Joe has now written another book, *Never A Time To Trust*, which deals with other aspects of his interesting life on Vancouver Island, still in many ways The Last Frontier. Throughout the book there is the strong thread of his fascination with cougars—remember that kid of nine whipping down that forest trail? It is about these animals that he has known, that others have known, and about the ways of Canada's most wily and vicious killer. They're all here, the loggers, the woodsmen, the do-gooders, the law makers, the bounty hunters and the men who administer the often wacky game regulations. They're here in their various and true colours.

There is a lot of Joe in this book. A man must write about

12

what he knows and in a lot of living in 75 years Joe Garner has learned a lot about Joe Garner.

There is no baloney in *Never A Time To Trust*. There is a lot of good red meat.

Barry Broadfoot
September 15, 1984

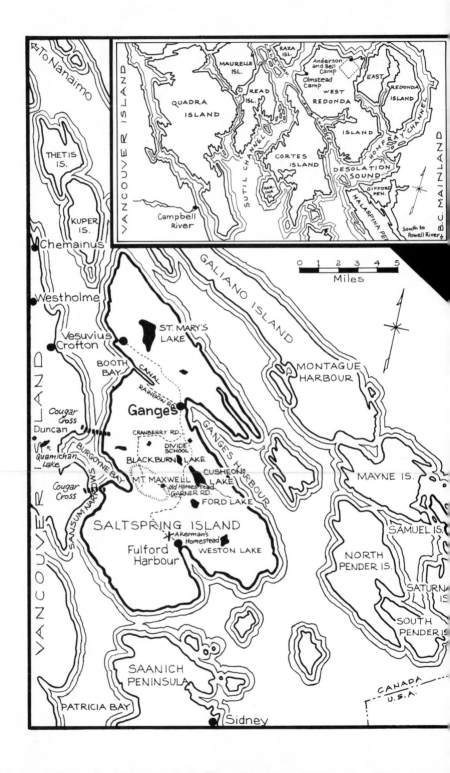

Pulling Together

Halfway between Ganges and Fulford Harbour on Salt-spring Island, the Garners owned 160 acres of mountainside. There were small patches of open land but we had no clearing of more than five acres.

By August of 1918 seven children had been born and all but the toddlers helped scratch out a living, one way or another.

Ethel had just turned 13. She worked for the Justice family and only got home on Sundays. Tom, 11, had a summer job in a small sawmill. I was nine that year—big enough to milk our three cows, help with the haying and give mother a hand with the barn chores. Margaret, seven, helped around the house but her main task was minding her two younger sisters. Pearl was four and Edie was two. They kept Marg on her toes every daylight minute. Oliver, the baby, was a husky breast-fed boy of four months. We knew that Mother would be 34 on August 13, but could not figure a way to give her a birthday party.

Dad was away working in Vancouver. The hours were never long enough for her to finish all the things she needed to do. Cooking, washing, and mending. There was the big vegetable garden. Her outdoor work alone was unending, with four pigs, a flock of chickens, several calves, 50 sheep and their lambs all to be fed. The worst was the horse, a mean cayuse named Dan Patch with the disposition of a camel. He had bitten Mother in June and her arm still bore the mark.

There had to be a trip to Ganges to shop at Mouat's store once a month. She and I would harness the horse after breakfast and hitch him to the buggy. That was the worst part. He was mean. Taking along baby Ollie she would drive the five miles to the village and usually get back to the farm about mid-afternoon.

We had so little money Mother arranged with the store to barter for the groceries we needed. Home-made butter and eggs by the dozen were main items for exchange. During the summer, there would be fresh fruits and vegetables. Sometimes we would butcher a sheep or a calf to trade for a barrel of flour or a hundred-pound sack of sugar.

It didn't seem to matter how much produce she took, Mother always said the same thing when she got home, "Had to skimp a bit to make ends meet but we'll get by."

This was her gentle way of warning us not to expect too many treats. We all knew well she never forgot to bring each of us a special little present every time she came home.

The six of us would be waiting to greet her. First, Mother would hand baby Ollie to Margaret while I held Dan Patch by the bit so he couldn't bite. Margaret would hurry into the house, flip Ollie onto his bed and rush back to help unload. The back end of the buggy was only a few steps from the kitchen door. Big or little, we all had jobs that fit our size.

There was always a kiss and a few jelly beans for Pearl and

18

Edie the minute Mother stepped from the buggy. She always managed to have the same colours and the same number for each. That way there would be no great fuss about who had the most or the prettiest. Usually there would be black licorice sticks for the older ones.

After everything was unloaded, I would lead that stubborn horse to the barn, back in the buggy, turn him out to pasture and rush back to find out what Mother had brought me. This shopping spree, I knew, had been a special one. I don't know why, I just felt it somehow.

"It's almost like Christmas!" Margaret whispered to me as I stepped into the kitchen. The big table was stacked with bags and boxes. There was more than I had ever seen.

"What's the big deal?" I asked Mother, trying to look unconcerned.

She sank into her chair and spread her arms on the table. Before answering, she opened her purse and fished out a small package wrapped in brown paper.

"Here's what I brought you, Joe," she said, and I tore off the paper. A beautiful pearl-handled pocket knife! My old one had been lost in the haymow a week ago.

"Thanks, Mom," I yelled and ran from the room out to the grindstone. In five minutes I had honed both blades razor sharp. Dad had taught me this skill so I could sharpen scythe blades.

Mother was sipping coffee while the children were relishing store-bought coconut cookies with milk. When I came in, Mother announced: "We are going to move to a new house at Ganges in September. Yo' Daddy thinks the schools will be better there, so he'll be home from the city to help us haul all our things down before school starts after the holidays. Said he's quitt'n his job then."

"Why all the raisins and coconut and candied fruit?" Margaret asked.

"We'll be having three parties all in one come next Sunday. Ethel, your birthday was missed. Mine is comin' this week and because we've lived here for so long we'll have us a goin' away party, too. I'm goin' to bake us three different kinds of cakes, fry up scads of chicken and fix all sorts of nice things. It will be a good way to remember leaving the farm when we get older. We'll make this a celebration almost as nice as Christmas."

There was a rustle under the table. Margaret found Pearl and Edie with the package of shredded coconut. Pearl had poked a slit through the paper and the two of them were pulling out long white strings of coconut. Margaret took away the package while Mother laid down the law to her protesting youngsters.

"Won't be no party if you two keep eating all the goodies," and told Marg to put all the food on the highest pantry shelf.

Everyone was busy getting things ready to move for the rest of the week. Tom and I boned out and cut up a deer I got with the old shotgun. This was packed in Mason jars, cooked, sealed and then put away in boxes. Ethel came home Saturday evening and helped make cakes and bread. Tom and Pearl filled the big box with dry firewood. The smells coming from the kitchen kept my stomach growling.

Sunday was party time. The day was hot, just right for swimming in our dammed-up pool in the creek below the house. Hidden away were the presents and birthday cards that we had made for Ethel and Mother. Tom had trotted five miles to the store and bought each of them a box of chocolates. I had done the milking early while Tom finished the evening chores. Margaret had churned butter so there was plenty of fresh buttermilk.

Dad had come from Vancouver on the old *Otter*, the slowest steamship on the Pacific coast. He walked from Ganges and arrived just after six o'clock. He was hungry as a bear. The scrumptious meal was served out on the shady part of the big porch. That feast was one I'll remember for as long as I live. We had stuffed ourselves and then Dad played his banjo and we all sang until dark. He then took the two little girls on his knee and told us Uncle Remus stories, saving our favourite, *Br'er Rabbit and the Briar Patch* for the last.

After Pearl and Edie were put to bed the rest of us gathered round the table to plan our big move. Two weeks from tonight we would be getting ready to sleep in our new house at Ganges. Dad and Mother discussed what furniture should be left and which animals to herd into town.

"I have bought a big stove with a water reservoir and a warming oven. This is already in the kitchen. There will be three new beds with real mattresses and blankets in the upstairs bedrooms when I go down there tomorrow."

"I'm sure glad you bought a bigger stove," Mother sighed. "This one will be good enough for the summers up here. We will only have to take our double bed, the small table and the chairs. The big table and benches can stay here. That will make it a lot easier when we come back next summer to put up fruit and do the haying. We should get a team and wagon to help that day, Oland," Mother suggested.

"Ted Akerman was on the boat and he offered his team and big wagon for two days. He'll be here early Saturday and go all day Sunday if we need him," Dad assured her.

"Can Tillie and Jim come up and help?" Tom asked.

"Don't see why not," Dad answered. "Why don't you go down and ask them? We could sure use some extra hands for the day."

Tom was blushing; he had a crush on Tillie.

"Three trips should do it."

"Only if we get all the stuff well packed and ready to go," Mother emphasized.

"What about the chickens and cows?" I asked.

"We'll take our best cow and about 25 chickens—no room for any more there," Mother reasoned, then added, "Maybe we'd better leave Dan Patch here? Or sell him?" she said, hopefully.

"No one on Saltspring would be dumb enough to buy that ornery cuss!" Tom exploded. "I'd be glad to ride him back up here and lock him safe in the pasture!"

"Ethel and I can go down and have lunch ready by the time the second load gets there," smiled Mother. "We should have the beds made up before dark. It will be so nice to sleep in a new house."

"I'll be able to help," Ethel said. "Mrs. Justice has arranged with Mrs. Crofton for me to work at Harbour House starting September. I think that was real nice of her."

"What about your job, Tom?" Dad asked.

"Mr. Justice has a small guest cottage. He said I can use that to sleep in and have my meals in his big house. I can come home Sundays, anyhow."

"Looks like everything is pretty well set then," Dad agreed, standing up to announce it was about bedtime.

"You know something?" Tom added, "Captain Justice told me today that he's heard the war could be over before winter sets in. Wouldn't that be great?"

"So I heard in Vancouver," Dad answered. "And they're not taking any more men for the army. I tried to sign up last week. That's how I know." In our excitement, this casual remark went unnoticed.

"Sure would be nice to see the three Seymour boys again," Mother mused, "but for now, let's get some sleep. Off to bed, everyone."

*   *   *

Times were tough just before the war ended. Prices were rising steadily. Wages, if they moved at all, were in a decline. I remember going shopping with Mother and Dad just after our move from the farm. We had picked and brought down boxes of plums and pears for winter. Mother needed 100 pounds of sugar and two dozen quart sealer jars. We had 24 dozen eggs to trade. Mr. Harris, the store manager, offered us 45¢ per dozen, almost double the price we had hoped for.

"That should about cover the sugar and jars," Dad beamed.

"No, it won't," Mr. Harris advised. "Price of white sugar has doubled since you were here last. One hundred pounds of white will cost you $22.00, the brown is $19.50. Don't forget that eggs were only two bits a dozen then."

"We need the sugar now. I'll take the brown and pay you the difference," Dad concluded grudgingly.

"Don't know what's happening to our world," Mother said when we got home. "We bought sugar for less than 10 cents a pound only a few months ago," she added, handing me a scoop. "Here, you put it in the bin so you'll always remember what 20¢ sugar looks like."

After days of hard work, plus all the picking and preparation, we ended up with dark, slightly bitter jar after jar of fruit for our winter desserts. Brown sugar turned out to be a poor way to save a couple of dollars.

For the next five years, our family lived like a troupe of gypsies. Every summer as soon as school was out Mother would pack blankets and dishes for our two months at the farm. Our holidays were mostly work. We picked fruit and put up hay seven days a week.

To make the move during the first two years we had Dan Patch hitched to our democrat. Rachael, our amiable Jersey cow, was tied in the rear and seemed to enjoy the walk.

Small wonder that folks meeting us would smile. There we

were, a jumpy cayuse hauling a rig with Mother and Dad plus a couple of kiddies perched on the only seat and three or four young Garners squeezed into the back with the chickens and other household goods. Tom and I walked, one on either side of the cow, to keep her horns from getting caught up in the spokes. There were the two white terriers scouting ahead. Meeting another rig on the narrow road was a challenge. The dogs would set up a great barking. Dan Patch would baulk, try gyrating about or whatever else came into his stupid mind. Tom and I would work at keeping the cow calm and we hoped Dad could straighten out the mess before that fool horse put us into the ditch or over a bank. There was seldom time for much more than a wave at passing neighbours.

Tom and I had two other important duties. From our house in Ganges up to what was known as the "Divide" was a narrow road climbing almost 1,000 feet in just over a mile. There were some short flat parts but mostly it was uphill. Dan Patch would get winded. We would stop for a short rest at least 10 times and, if it was very hot, he would have to stop up to 20 times. Dad had made what we called chocks. These were tapered cedar blocks like a steep wedge, about a foot long. They were eight inches high at one end, six inches wide, then tapered to one inch thick on the end to shove under the wheels. When the horse stopped we shoved a chock under the high rear wheels. We then stepped to the front side and stood on one of the wooden spokes. This held the wagon from slipping back.

Dad, Margaret and Pearl would get off and walk up the steeper hills. Dad would give Mother the reins. He would snap a lead rope onto the bit and walk ahead to lead the baulky critter.

When the caravan started again we picked up the chocks and went back to minding the unconcerned cow.

At the top of Divide hill, we started down a half mile of road even steeper and far more dangerous. We had a chain bolted to each side of the wagon box. A hook on the end of each chain had been made in Bill McAfrie's blacksmith shop and it fitted over a spoke to stop the wheel from turning. We called this a "rough-lock." When the chain was hooked the wheel just slid along on its steel rim.

Dad would climb back onto the narrow wagon seat, take the reins from Mother and give Tom and me our final instructions. I always took the right-hand side of the wagon. This was the dangerous side.

"Boys, watch my hands carefully. When I put up my right hand you snap that hook onto a spoke," he would say to me. "If you do it too soon we will be stuck, and if done too late we will be in a runaway. Tom, you do the same when my left hand goes up."

With both back wheels locked, it didn't matter where the cow put her horns. When the wagon was past the worst part, Dad would stop and back up enough for Tom to take the hook off my side. We would go another quarter mile to the bottom of the hill and Tom would unlock the other wheel.

The road on the south side of the Divide hill had been graded with pick and shovel. It was so narrow three turnouts had to be built so wagons could pass if they met on this steep section. The cut banks on the top side were up to five feet high while the dropoff on the low side was sometimes over 15 feet. There had been a serious accident near the top when a team couldn't hold the load and everything rolled over the bluff on the low side.

"Three people almost killed right here," Dad would always point out to impress on us how important it was to get the chains and chocks in place properly. There were four more hills where we had to chain the wheels on the way to the farm. The chocks were used dozens of times. Tom and I

were proud to accept the danger as well as the responsi-
bilities of these trips.

There was only one real farm between Ganges and our
turnoff. The Conrey dairy farm was near Blackburn's Lake
on the south side of the Divide hill.

The rest of the places were nothing but small clearings
between the rock benches or near the creek bottoms. That
was poor land for farming. People on them worked hard for
almost no return.

Grouse Hunting on Saltspring

It was the fall of 1923. Dad invited Jim Dalziel and his brother Bill over to the old homestead for a grouse hunt. The Dalziels owned and operated a box factory as part of their small sawmill in Victoria. We had cut some logs for export to Japan, but this market had come to an end in the spring. Logs cut for export were in lengths that did not suit most mills. There was considerable waste. The Japanese specified all logs must be cut in multiples of 6′ 6″.

Because the box factory used all sorts of short lengths, Dalziel's was the only place for our boom to be processed. Tom and I knew Dad was anxious to sell our last boom. We knew Dad was smart too.

As youngsters during the 'teens and early twenties on Saltspring Island we grew up with blue grouse. The island was a haven for the large good-eating birds. We had our favourite hunting spots. We could get as many grouse as we could pack home every time we went after them.

Every spring as we tended sheep and brought in the cows

to be milked we would listen for the hooting of the male grouse. The woods around our old farm would throb with the WHOO WHOO WHOO's of these "hooters."

Sitting on logs, stumps or branches of trees, they would fan out their great tails, fluff out their feathers, and bare a large yellow spot on their necks. During the mating ritual the males strutted about like turkey gobblers. One, two or sometimes three females would be sitting on a nest of eight to 12 speckled brown eggs not far away.

Unmolested, most of these eggs hatched in late April or early May. We always marvelled at the way the tiny yellow chicks with darkish spots on their backs could scamper about, then swiftly hide, motionless. Even with scant ground cover it was hard to find them. Their protection was the camouflage nature had given them. The southern slopes of the dry ridges was where we found most nests.

Predators, such as domestic cats gone wild and ravens, were not nearly as numerous then as they are today. One day we watched a pair of adult ravens catch and eat a covey of eight chicks. Another day Tom killed a raven with three young grouse in its crop. When ravens find young grouse they will not leave until they have bolted down the last one. We hated these black monsters with a passion.

The hunting season opened around September 15. This was the most exciting time of the year. Hunting was great sport but it also supplied us with some of our winter's meat. When any game was killed the meat was eaten fresh or salted or canned, depending on the weather and need. Mother wasted little.

Tom drove our one-ton model-T Ford, with solid tires on the rear wheels, to Fulford Harbour to meet Walter Curley's launch. The Curleys were our friends and neighbours. Dad had arranged with Walter to bring the Dalziels from Saanich on Vancouver Island to Saltspring. Our guests would arrive early Friday evening. Dad gave me a note to the teacher to excuse me from the Ganges school at noon. I jogged the five miles home and had time to bag and clean six young grouse for supper.

Mother had arrived earlier from Ganges. She and baby Oliver, with several boxes of supplies, had ridden up with Tom and Dad on their way to Fulford. Tom had put fresh milk and cream in the creek to cool. By six o'clock, we were feasting on fried grouse, home-cured bacon, fresh butter spread over hot bread. There were two wild blackberry pies, a real treat.

At supper, Jim Dalziel asked me to hunt with him the next day. I was so excited when I saw the beautiful guns these men had that I stayed awake for the best part of the night, or so I imagined. They each had a new double-barreled Parker with spring ejectors. Tom was to use his old lever action 12-gauge.

"Joe," Dad snapped at me, "you can use the ten-gauge with the store-bought shells. Think you can handle it?"

"Sure can," I shot back.

I would show them! The old gun was missing its cocking apparatus. We had fashioned a single link cut from a heavy otter trap chain to reset the firing mechanism. This link was tied to the gun stock with a short piece of a leather shoelace. It fit the square bit of protruding steel like a short wrench to cock the gun. The Dalziels asked if they could try the ten-gauge on a tossed can. It kicked them so hard one shot each was enough.

Jim looked at me, then at the gun, smiled, and asked, "You going to use that cannon?"

"Sure am," I assured him. The end of the barrel was above the level of my eyes when the stock rested on the ground.

"Don't fret yourself about Joe," Tom advised.

"Would you like a try with one of our guns?" Jim asked. "There's still enough light to try it."

"Sure would!" Tom had been hoping for this offer.

Showing him how to release the safety and then familiarizing him with the other new gadgets, Jim handed him the gun and a couple of shells. I stood well back, holding a small condensed milk can.

"Let 'er go!" Tom ordered, with a wave of his hand. He hit it once on the way up and again on the way down.

Dad looked at the can. There were more holes than can left.

"Looks like a sieve," he said. "You hit a grouse that hard, it will hardly be fit for stew," and he tossed the can in the trash barrel. "Not a bit of use to waste more shells on such foolishness."

Abruptly, he went on into the house to get ready for bed.

Next morning Jim and I were away as soon as it was light enough to shoot. Jim had a well-trained springer spaniel, so I guided him south toward Lee's Mountain. This was good country for a spaniel. Open ridges with plenty of salal patches in between. There would be a covey of grouse in almost every patch. Spot, his brown and white pooch, was kept so busy retrieving birds he was almost exhausted by eight o'clock.

"We're heading for Walters' Spring. Your dog can get a drink there and we can have a sandwich," I suggested.

"Let's count our birds, too," Jim said, then asked, "How come it's called Walters' Spring?"

"Because, sir, Mr. Walters used to live in that log cabin we just passed. Mrs. Walters had to pack water from the spring during dry spells. Trouble was, the cougars from around Maxwell's Peak drank there too."

"Did you know the Walters?"

30

"Dad, Tom and I were looking for our sheep when Dad called in to chat. I remember that meeting."

"'Howdy!' Walters greeted us. 'How's the Garners?'

"'Howdy! How are things going?' Dad asked.

"'Wife up and left a week ago. Says she won't live in this wilderness any longer. Big cougar followed her right to the door. Scared hell out of her. I was away to the store. She was all packed up when I got home.'"

"That was more than five years ago." I explained to Jim. "The cougars still come here to drink. See those fresh tracks?"

"Well, I'll be damned!" said Jim, surprised.

After our snack and a cold drink from the spring, we counted our bag. We had 22 blues and one willow.

"These are getting pretty heavy to carry," Jim said. "Let's string them up in the shade. We can come by here on the way home."

"Okay," I agreed. "Anyhow, the best hunting is just over the hill."

"Better than what we've had?"

"For sure! Let's go get 'em," and I was already up, impatient to get going.

In the next clearing Spot ranged far out and up the hill above us. We heard him let out a "Yip," and saw two grouse sailing downhill about 40 yards ahead. Jim fired twice and the last bird dropped.

Now the old ten-gauge roared. The lead bird folded. I regained my balance from the recoil and Jim was looking at me with a strange expression.

"I don't believe what I've just seen," he exclaimed and he paced off the distance to the dead grouse. It was 70 yards.

"Don't spoil the birds too badly at that range," I said in explanation.

"You kill birds that far often?" Jim asked in disbelief.

31

"Sure do. Tiny Seymour taught me how to lead and shoot. He was a famous sniper in the war," I explained, and I told him Tiny was my idol. One of the best shots in Canada. Weighed about 300 pounds. Stood just over 6′ 7″!

Half an hour later, another chance came for me. Another clean kill. It was a full 60-yard shot that can only be done with a full chock ten-gauge! Dalziel took the gun, looked first at me, then at this dilapidated old firing piece. He said not a word but he kept making clucking noises with his tongue.

The sun was plenty warm. Spot's tongue lolled out. Our pack sacks were again heavy and our shells almost gone.

"Maybe we should angle back toward our birds," Jim suggested. Spot, first at the spring, almost drank it dry and then sprawled in the shade of a big log. We had 38 blue grouse and the one willow.

"Is there a limit here?" Jim questioned.

"We never shoot more than we can carry home."

The last of the hunters to arrive at the farm, we were greeted by Dad. Two nice bucks were hanging in the wood-shed.

"Where did you get the deer?" asked Jim.

"All the shooting and racket you fellers were making! All I had to do was keep quiet and watch the deer trails until the right one came along. You must have spooked out a dozen good bucks. I couldn't keep count."

Tom and Bill Dalziel had brought in 36 blues. They had hunted to the north of us, finding some grouse in the Dry Lake clearing back of the old Carter farm. There was another spring between Dry Lake and Maxwell's Peak.

"We had lunch at the spring and then hunted out along the open ridges where all those oak trees are," Tom explained.

"That's tough shooting when those big blues sail from the trees going downhill," Bill commented.

"Thought there was a war over there by the amount of shooting you two were doing," Jim teased.

"We were only getting about one bird for every three shots," Bill complained.

"Say, Tom, did you go down to those cougar caves?" Dad asked.

"Not me!" Bill retorted ruefully, "No cougar's gonna have me for lunch, then scatter my bones! How did you know about those cougar anyhow, Oland?"

"We were there two years ago. There was a litter of kittens and the mother living in that big cave," said Dad. "Ed Lee helped me lower that tree trunk down the entrance hole. While he stood guard with his rifle, I climbed down 15 feet to look back into the den. Found a fresh sheep carcass that had been dragged in. Partly eaten. In the gravel there were big tracks and lots of smaller ones. That stench of rotting meat and cougar manure was so strong it hurt your eyes. Didn't actually see any cougars but I could hear them moving farther back in the caves. No place for a man to be without a gun," Dad concluded.

We were all tired and thirsty. Casually, as though it hadn't been planned, Dad produced a cooled gallon jug of Saltspring Island's best apple cider. On the veranda the men relaxed in the shade, drank cider and discussed guns, politics and the bounty on predators and Dad seemed anxious to remind Jim of the rights of farmers, trappers and prospectors.

"They were permitted to shoot game for food any time, and I can tell you one thing, we would have starved here if we couldn't have shot some game during those first few years."

"Did you know that cougars are classified as vermin?" Jim asked.

"I think 'varmint' is a better name for those killers," Dad said quickly. "Having sheep I just naturally hate all cougar."

"The first year that the free farmer's licence confined the farmer to hunting only on his own land was 1918," Dad informed us. "What about cougar bounties, Jim?"

"Beginning in 1920," Jim replied, "hunters owning good hounds were encouraged by the government game department to destroy all cougar. The bounty was raised to $40. There were 372 shot last year. Some of the better hunters made well over $1,000. You know, that makes last year a record for the most cougar shot."

"And you can't trust any one of those devils," Dad stated. "Do you remember seven years ago this month a panther attacked and almost killed two children at Cowichan Lake?"

"I know the Ashburnam family well. It was their daughter Doreen and her friend, Tony Farrer that the cougar jumped on. They were goin' along a trail to get their pony. Tony was carrying the bridle. It was in some woods where they spotted this panther crouched on a log. When they turned and started to run for home the big cat sprang on Doreen, knocking her to the ground. Tony rushed in and began beating it over the head with the bridle. Then it left Doreen and knocked young Tony over backwards. Talk about a couple of plucky kids! Doreen picked up the bridle and continued beating the snarling animal." Jim paused. "Actually, it was the Ashburnam's little dog that saved the children by attacking the cougar's butt. It whirled on the dog knocking it some 20 feet into the salal. While it was going after the dog the kids escaped and made it home."

"I've heard several versions to how this all ended, Jim," Dad said. "Now, can you tell us just what did happen?"

"There were some reliable people involved," Jim explained, "Mr. Marsh and old Dad Caldwell hunted and killed the panther. A doctor from Duncan was rushed in from the south end of the lake. You know, it took 36 stitches just to close the gashes on Tony's head. That little dog was sewn up like a patchwork quilt. As for Marsh and Caldwell," Jim went on, "they shot the cougar only 'bout 100 yards from where it had fought with the children. Strange as it may seem, that old tom was completely blind. When it tried to run from the dogs it banged head-on into several trees. Then it turned and fought.

"After the doctor finished stitching up the children they asked him to do an autopsy on the cougar. He said the animal was old and about ready to die from starvation."

"Suppose you fellows know," Bill added, "that both youngsters were honoured by the Governor General of Canada with a Royal Albert Medal for their bravery. Only last week I talked with Doreen. She's 18 now. A beautiful young lady."

"It was the Ashburnan affair that made us realize that panthers were a real menace to our children," said Dad. "We told all our youngsters what to do if they met one. As a matter of fact, without those instructions Joe probably wouldn't be here."

"How do you figure that?" Jim asked, looking sharply at Dad.

"It was less than a year later that a big panther chased Joe for almost half a mile! Took out after him near the bottom of the hill and didn't give up until he had this house in sight. Come on to the end of the veranda and I'll show you," Dad urged, and we looked down over the small hay meadow, about two acres of flat land less that 50 yards from the house.

Dad pointed, "See that old stump near the rail fence at the south end? That's where the panther stopped and crouched in the high grass to watch as Joe came up the hill toward home."

"You believe it was the sight of the house that stopped the beast?"

"Not entirely, Jim," Dad explained. "We had our big

35

black dog tied to the cedar there. Chain was fastened to that crooked root. There would be a fair commotion when Blackie jumped over the root and began barking. I believe it was all that noise that caused the panther to turn aside."

"That old dog would go crazy if there was a strange cat or coon around. That's why we kept him tied," Tom explained.

"How old were you when all this happened?" Jim asked.

"I was only eight and a half then. Just over six years ago. I was on my way home with some groceries from Mouat's store. It was getting dark when the panther went across the road in front of me."

"You afraid?" asked Bill.

I tried to control a shudder. The memory of that terrifying chase was as clear as if it had happened only yesterday. I was embarrassed to talk about it when either Dad or strangers were around. I couldn't go on.

Tom understood and came to my rescue.

"Jim, if you would like to go with Joe first thing in the morning, he could show you exactly where everything happened. I can take Bill to the tree where Dad and I shot the other cougar the following year. Won't take more'n an hour to do both," Tom suggested.

"Dandy with me," Bill nodded.

Jim smiled in agreement, then added, "Think we should take our guns in case we see some grouse?"

"You are pretty sure to put up birds at both places. You can't shoot without a gun and that's what we're here for," Dad reminded them.

Just then Mother called, "Supper's ready. I thought it might be nicer to eat out on the porch where it's cool."

Ethel, my oldest sister, was smiling as she set the last plate on the big plank table. There was fried young grouse and Mother's famous sweet milk gravy on hot biscuits. Bowls of garden-fresh vegetables and a dozen ears of corn. Ethel had made a deep peach plum pie, topped with thick Jersey cream and served in our porridge bowls. The Dalziels beamed. Everyone was in a good mood.

After the meal Jim and Bill lit up their pipes and relaxed. I watched Jim's every move as he put the tobacco in the bowl then poked it a bit with his index finger. When he lit it with a match, then blew out a cloud of smoke, I made plans to get me one.

When the dishes were washed and put away Tom drove Ethel, Mother and young Oliver down to Ganges. He was back in less than an hour.

"That T-model sure beats horses," he laughed.

After breakfast next morning Jim and I headed down across the little hay meadow. Now I could talk freely about my narrow escape. Where the road entered the meadow we stopped on the downhill side.

"Take a good look at the gate from here. I had to jump over it with the panther not 20 feet behind me," I said.

Jim looked at the gate, then at me and said, "At eight years old that gate would be higher than your head." There was a note of disbelief in his voice.

"We can go down the trail the way the panther came up, then come back on the road I ran up that day," I suggested.

"Sounds good to me," and we walked about 100 feet to where the trail took off to the right.

"This is where that big cat tried to cut me off from the house. I was right here when he splashed across the creek."

Jim stood for a minute looking first up at the gate, then down to where the trail crossed just below a big pool, then back at me. He made several clucking noises with his tongue. There was silence as he followed me along the trail. Spot soon took a hot scent and flushed a big hooter.

Jim got the bird with a single shot. As he shoved it into his bag, he asked, "How much farther to where you first met your friend?"

"We're over halfway there now."

Jim was looking up at the big fir trees and said, "This is really nice timber. If you ever want to put it in the water, we'll buy it from you at top prices."

"We won't forget the offer," I assured him, pleased as punch that I was the first to know.

A few more minutes down the trail, we could see the old road to our left. Stopping by a huge fir stump I sat down on the moss on one side of the trail. Jim sat across from me.

"This is the spot, right here, where that big panther crouched to watch me."

"We're not more than 20 feet from where you had to walk past him," Jim observed. "How scared were you? How did you feel at eight years old?"

"I was so scared, it was like being in a trance or a real bad dream. My hair felt like it was standing on end, especially along the back of my neck. My head was throbbing. I remembered the words Dad had told me a year before. 'Never Run—Never Run. Walk slowly toward home. Bang two rocks together as loud as you can. The noise may save you.' Truthfully, Jim, I moved like a wound-up tin toy soldier. Come on down and I will demonstrate for you."

We scrambled down the steep side-hill, then walked down the grade for about 40 yards. We stood to look up the road.

"This is the spot where I first saw the panther." I picked up two rocks and started banging them together, demonstrating just what I had done six years earlier.

As we walked up the road toward home Jim followed, watching my every move from about five feet back. I continued banging the rocks, louder and louder. We came to the trail where we both slid down the bank. I stopped and looked at him.

"This was the toughest place to get by. The desire to run became so great that it was almost impossible to just keep on walking."

Fifty yards ahead we came to the bridge that crossed the creek. The memory came back.

"When I looked back from here six years ago I saw that panther turn and start to run up the same trail we just now came down. I dropped the rocks and made a run for the gate. Almost a quarter mile from here. My bare feet flew up the slopes. Never did wear shoes in the summertime. My feet were tough as leather."

"Why did you start to run from here?"

"You can't be chased from behind if the enemy is ahead. I felt sure that the big danger was ahead. I had to get to the gate first."

We walked on up the road, then sat on a log for a breather about two-thirds of the way along.

"Could you see the bastard on the other side of the creek as you ran?" Jim asked.

"No, but I could sure hear him crashing through the salal. We were travelling at about the same speed."

When we were again at the trail below the gate, we stopped.

"Do you believe that humans can sometimes have supernatural powers?" I asked.

"I don't know for sure," Jim said hesitantly. "I've heard tell of strange things happening if your life is in danger."

"Six years ago, I was running as fast as I could, or so I thought, until I looked down there and saw this devil charging toward me. Its mouth was open enough to show its big fangs. Right here something snapped. Everything seemed to go into slow motion. My stride increased by more than three times normal. My feet barely touched the ground. Almost like flying.

"When I came to the gate I seemed to have just sailed over it like a swallow on a windy day. I scurried some 30 yards farther. Collapsed in a heap in the tall grass. I heard Blackie barking at the top of his lungs. Then I felt safe. You know, Jim, I was so exhausted my legs wouldn't carry me. It took three tries before I was able to stand and go up to the house.

"I must have been white as a ghost. Tom said so. He asked me, 'What's the matter?'"

"'Big panther chased me up the road and almost caught me at the gate.'"

"Dad and Tom got their guns, untied Blackie and rushed down to the field. The dog chased the cat out from under some windfall logs but they both missed."

Jim looked at me for a full minute before he spoke.

"Hard story to believe," he said, then added, "Think you can jump the gate right now?"

"Hold this ten-gauge for me and watch," and I handed him the gun, took off my hunting bag and dropped it at my feet, bent over to tighten my sneaker laces, and then I started the run at the gate.

I had been making this jump for a year. It was more fun than opening and closing the damn thing. I had it down pat. I jumped it cleanly and went back to get the bag and gun. Jim was just standing there. He appeared to be a bit stunned.

He said, "This has to be one for Ripley's *Believe It Or Not*."

"That panther was a ground fighter," I explained. "He stayed to kill two sheep and a deer right in sight of our house. Tom and Dad tried to get him with our dog. He would not tree. He fought with Blackie and almost tore one of his ears off. The Collins family had hounds so Dad asked them to come and help. After a long chase, that devil killed one of their hounds, then climbed a tree. They shot him and opened his stomach. It contained both deer and sheep meat plus parts of a raccoon.

"Mother made sure the smaller children stayed inside

until they dragged that killer into the barnyard. That's exactly how it happened," I concluded.

About noon, Tom drove our guests to Fulford Harbour in the Model-T, loaded with two nice bucks and over 50 grouse. As the launch was pulling away from the wharf, Jim shouted, "Send that boom down to our mill tomorrow, Oland!"

Dad yelled okay. We stood and waved them good-bye. Tom and I exchanged knowing nods. When the cheque came for the logs it was for $100.00 more than the agreed price.

"That's how you sell logs when the market is down," Tom told me.

"Pretty nice way," I agreed, thinking of the grouse shoot.

Jim and Bill came the next year. Our first hunting trip started a friendship that lasted almost a lifetime.

A Walk Into Bighorn Country

Three years after meeting the Dalziels, we left Saltspring Island. In May of 1926 Mother had her last child. Dr. Sutherland warned her it would be fatal if she were to get pregnant again. She chose the only way out.

It was agreed Mother would take eight children and move to Vancouver. Dad would stay on Saltspring and keep Pearl and Oliver with him. Tom and I built Mother a house in East Vancouver that summer.

Tom and I didn't like the big city. There was no place to fish or hunt. The next year we two moved to Westholme on Vancouver Island. We met the Holmans there. Dolph and Henry became our instant hunting and fishing buddies.

In 1948, seven of us decided to form a hunting club. Tom had his pilot's licence and I was about ready for mine. With an aircraft on floats, wilderness areas became much more accessible. We located, surveyed, and bought land where we built log cabins in two isolated areas. One was in the high country to the south of Chilco Lake. This was mountain goat and bighorn sheep territory. The second cabin was near Rosita Lake in some of the finest moose country in the world.

Tom and I were now 30 years older than when first we had hunted on Saltspring but each fall brought with it the same enthusiasm and anticipation we'd known as youngsters.

Don Butt called the yearly meeting of the Duncan Rosita Gun Club for September 1, 1954, at the Tzouhalem Hotel. Present were Tom, Ted Robson, Brad Harrison, Bill Auchinachie, Gordon MacDonald, Don and myself. The main reason for the meeting was to set up times and dates for our annual Chilcotin hunting trip. We decided to leave October 27 at about noon. We would meet at Tom's house for a final check, then drive the 30 miles north to catch the 2 p.m. ferry leaving Nanaimo for Vancouver. Next would be the 200 mile drive up the Fraser Canyon and on to Clinton and then 60 miles west to the Gang Ranch. We would camp in the high country above Churn Creek.

"If I'm going to get the beer, groceries, and other gear, I should know for sure how many are going this year," Don said. "Hands up those taking a guest. Okay, that makes 12 in all."

The guests were Syro (George Syrotuck), Johnny Ames, General Jimmy Watt (U.S. Marines), Gary (my nephew) and Bert Bennett.

"Bert is willing to take on the job of cook, just to be along," Don Butt explained.

"With 12 people in camp, he is going to be the busiest and most important person on this trip," Tom remarked casually.

He handed Don a hundred dollars, asking "Will that be enough to take care of our supplies?"

"If we all dub in that much it should just about cover everything, including gas and ferry."

Don had been our "banker" for the past 10 years and he knew what was needed. Small but essential items such as needle and thread, gas-lantern mantles, matches, first aid kit, soap and such like were always there when we set up camp. And, yes, there would be several rolls of toilet paper.

"Which vehicles do we want to take?" Bill asked.

"We have a new Volkswagen van. She'll carry a ton and keep everything dry. With chains and a hand winch it's real good in rough going," I offered.

"I've overhauled the winch on my half-ton so it's ready," Don added.

"The ¾-ton pickup has new snow tires and is ready to go," Ted stated.

"For God sake, you fellows are offering all these fancy new machines. If it turns warm and rains we can be in real trouble without a four-wheel drive in that back country," Bill declared. "Anyone got a jeep?"

"We have that old army Jeep with a winch. It's getting a bit old and run down but can be ready if you think we can get it started in that cold weather," Tom offered.

"Throw a couple of extra batteries in the back and I'll be glad to give her a whirl," Bill said.

"That makes four rigs. We sure as hell don't need any more," Don said flatly as he closed his notebook.

"See you all at my place, ten o'clock on the 27th. I'll have the Jeep and Volkswagen ready. I'll put two barrels of extra gas in the Jeep," Tom said as he stood to go.

"Just one more problem to settle before we leave. I have to be at a meeting in Quesnel on October 28," I said.

"Got a plan?" Ted asked.

"If Tom and Bill handle the Jeep and Volkswagen I can drive to Quesnel in the station wagon. The secretary has to be there in any event. He can drop Gary and me off at the creek crossing near Augustine's old camp about 10 o'clock on the morning of October 29.

"Ted or I will be there to pick you up," Don promised.

"Just to be sure we don't forget the day and time, maybe a reminder note in each of our wallets would be a good idea?" Ted suggested.

We each wrote a note and tucked it in our billfold.

"We will be there on time if we have to drive all night," I assured them.

We left Quesnel about 10 p.m. on October 28 to drive south to 100 Mile House for a few hours sleep. We hadn't done more than 20 miles when we hit wet snow. Soon there was glare ice on the blacktop. We didn't get to 100 Mile House until hours later. Because of the weather we decided to keep going. We put the chains on. An hour later, after several complete spins, we had travelled only about 10 miles. We were now on the plateau that runs south to Clinton. We were able to travel without chains for a spell. We turned onto the Gang Ranch road and got out for a stretch. To the east there was a red glow in the sky.

"What the hell time is it?" Gary asked.

"My watch says 4:15 a.m.," Earl Reynolds said. "How long from here to Augustine's, Joe?"

The sky was clear. Frost sparkled where the headlights shone. I judged the temperature to be about zero.

"If the road is no worse than this we could be there in about four hours."

"Hell Joe! That gives us a couple of hours to play around. How about a beer to take up some of our leisure time," Gary suggested.

"Sure, but we'll drink it on the fly. All aboard!" I ordered.

When we reached the Fraser River Bridge the sun was up. It was 7:30. More than 30 miles of rough uphill slogging to

Augustine's. Half a mile past the bridge we hit glare ice and chained up again.

We crawled in low gear for the next few miles. There was a stretch of level road where we passed by the big bunk house and store buildings of the Gang's headquarters.

"Shall we take the chains off here?" suggested Earl.

"Too steep ahead. Best we just tighten them up and leave 'em on. We have to climb almost 2,000 feet in the next 10 miles."

They had never been over this part of the Cariboo before. The country had opened up into some of the finest grazing hills in all of North America. It stretched as far as the eye could see in every direction. It was rated the third largest ranch in the world.

As we ground our way up the steep grades Gary popped the caps off two more beer. It had turned to slushy ice and had to be held down by the car heater before it would flow out.

"Tomorrow you'll probably be having beersicles, if it gets any colder," I teased.

No one home at Augustine's. He was a local Indian and held a big game guiding licence. We had planned to have breakfast at his cabin.

"Probably out hunting with some American party," Earl suggested.

"That's not going to help the empty feeling in my stomach one little bit," Gary said, seriously.

We didn't find out about his wife and kids moving out to Clinton until later.

We drove on three more miles where the road crossed the creek and headed south toward Sheep Flats and Wikoff Meadows.

"This where Don and Ted are going to pick you up?" Earl asked.

"Yeah. They should be here in the next few minutes. I've got some sandwiches and a thermos of hot coffee in my bag."

"Let's eat while we wait. I'm about starved," Earl suggested, and by the time the coffee and food was finished it was well past ten.

"Do you suppose they could have forgotten?" Earl asked, anxiously.

"Not likely. They could have shot a deer on the way out and taken time to dress it. We all put a reminder note in our billfolds to be sure. It can be really serious when people don't keep a date in this country. At ten below zero you could freeze to death in half an hour."

"What do you want to do?" Earl asked.

"You better head for home. We'll be okay," I assured him, and we helped him take off the chains.

"How far to camp?" Gary asked, looking at his city shoes.

"Just under 20 miles the way this road twists around. There is no other way to get in or out, so we might as well start walking. We will probably meet the Jeep before we are a mile along. Why not get going?"

We watched Earl as he drove out of sight and shouldered our light packs. We headed south at a fast walk. We hadn't gone far when Gary stopped to tie up a broken shoelace.

"These damn oxfords are okay around the office. They sure as hell are no good on frozen ground," he remarked, disgustedly.

"Might as well keep going. Too damned cold to stand around," I told him and we agreed to try jogging for awhile. In my low street shoes and light socks my feet were already numb with the cold. By noon we realized we were going to have to walk into camp. The sun was out but it was bitter cold with a north wind. We broke ice at the edge of a small lake for a drink about two o'clock.

47

"Let's make a fire and warm up," Gary suggested.

"More than halfway there. It's only about eight miles from here," I encouraged, but I agreed to stop and we lit a dry stump to dry our wet shoes and socks. That fire felt so good, we found it hard to get mobile again. Gary stood up and announced, "Eight miles to go. Let's jog it before we starve."

At 4:30 two very tired and footsore men limped into camp. Ted and Don were sitting by the campfire. When they looked up and saw us standing there they both flushed red with embarrassment and blurted out together: "Sorry, we forgot!"

"So are we," was my frigid reply.

"Take these chairs while I fix you a hot rum," Ted offered, sheepishly. "Get off your ass, Don, and help me."

Don stood up, staring at our shoes which were falling off our feet. I kicked mine off and threw them into the campfire along with my light socks. Ted handed us steaming mugs of water and Eagle Brand condensed milk, laced with plenty of rum and a dash of cinnamon.

"Drink that before you decide to kill us," he said. We were cold, tired and about starved. That big mug of hot rum did more to patch up a suddenly shaky friendship than all the words in the dictionary could have.

Bert had made a monster stew which was simmering on the gas stove. By the time we had finished a second hot rum, devoured three bowls of stew and a loaf of bread things were looking up.

Gary looked at Don and said with a big grin, "Butt, you old son of a bee, you owe me a pair of dress shoes and a pair of socks soon as we get back to Duncan."

"We are here, we're happy," I shrugged, "so let's forget it ever happened."

When we got our cots and sleeping bags set up it was

starting to get dusk. Gary had changed into his hunting gear and was itching to get going.

"Try that timber to the south. Usually see something there about this time of day," Bill suggested. "Get going. Damn little daylight left."

It wasn't long until Gary walked proudly back into camp with a nice four-point buck humped on his back. It sure hadn't taken him long to recuperate.

"That's youth for you," Syro explained to the 'over 40's' as we sat around the fire.

*   *   *

Tom and Bill were the early risers. They had a big fire blazing an hour before daylight. We were going to hunt sheep. The season ended October 31 so we only had a couple of days to shoot a ram legally.

There were a fair number of sheep in the area. A band of more than 30 had been glassed on Sheep Flats from the ridges above by the gang who got in ahead of us.

"There are at least two big rams and about 20 ewes and lambs on those steep ridges above Wycott Meadows," Don said.

We ate hotcakes and bacon with three eggs on top. The chitchat was bighorn sheep and how we were going to hunt them. We drank our coffee. You could feel the excitement in everyone. An inch of fresh snow had fallen during the night. Ideal tracking and hunting conditions.

Everyone had a different idea as to what should be done and where to go. Don called for silence and asked Ted to come and stand with him. They'd pick teams.

"We're going to divide into two parties. Ted takes five to Sheep Flats. I'll take the rest to Wycoff."

"Pick your bunch first," Don said.

"Okay," Ted agreed, and called off Tom and Syro, then

Gary and me. "Jimmy Watt will hunt with me too."

"The rest of those wanting to hunt sheep, stand by the fire so we can see who's going to go where," Don ordered. Everybody stood but Bert, our cook.

"I put up a double lunch for everyone last night. In the box at the end of the table. Help yourselves when you are ready to go," said Bert and he began putting the dirty dishes in the big washtub while sipping his mug of steaming brew.

I fired up the Jeep and the men came aboard. We had hunted this area for six years. The previous year we had slashed a road leading to the top of the mountain. This saved almost 10 miles of walking to where the sheep grazed during the daytime. They left the lower meadows just after daylight to make their way up to the rockslides into the rough country. There were three trails leading from the timber on top to the meadows below. Ted and the general got off at the first trail. Tom and George took the second. Gary and I walked three miles past the end of the road to the last gully that led over the rimrock.

We were not the only hunters. Fresh cougar tracks in the snow. During the night a big cat had walked up to the trail we were planning to go down. Gary saw the tracks first and pointed, "That's no kitten."

"An old tom on the prowl. He could be watching us from the timber right now."

"Let's go after him."

"Nope! We are hunting sheep and nothing else."

The top of the mountain was just over 5,000 feet while the feeding meadows were about 2,000 feet lower. A lot of rough ups and downs during a day's hunt. We carried enough rope to ease ourselves over some of the steeper drop-offs.

It was now light enough to use our binoculars. On the rim, we sat to listen and glass below. We spotted several deer and then four ewes with three half grown lambs making their way along a trail toward the box canyon.

"No rams in that lot," I remarked, as we started on down the trail. The sight of the seven sheep had given Gary a slight attack of "buck fever." His hands were shaking. He had to rest against a tree to be able to look through his 7 x 35 binoculars.

"Well, I know what to look for from here on. Those are the first sheep I have ever seen in the wild," he said excitedly.

There were fresh tracks and droppings everywhere you looked. Ten minutes farther down the trail we walked out on a narrow precipice jutting out from the main mountainside. This crag was almost flat on top. It stuck out for 100 feet or more. Near its outer end, the sheer vertical drop was more than 200 feet to the rock slide below. We walked out to look around. The flat surface narrowed to less than four feet wide for the last 20 feet. We angled around some scrubby jack pines that obscured the outer end from the trail. I pointed to the hollows where sheep had lain for hundreds of years. The winds had blown the snow off this crag. "Four years ago when I looked out from these trees, two big rams stood up, gave me a glare and jumped over the edge."

Gary inched his way out to where the beds were.

"Wall-to-wall sheep manure," he said, grinning. Then he looked over the side.

"My God! That's over 100 feet straight down. Did they kill themselves?" he asked.

"Didn't even slow them up. When they landed in that loose shale they slid down for another 15 or 20 feet. Then trotted off toward that box canyon."

"Did you get a shot?"

"All I got was a dose of the shakes. Worse than you had a few minutes ago. I've had a disease called 'sheep fever' ever since those two rams looked me in the eye."

"Must have been a real thriller."

"This is the best lookout around. We'll keep in the trees for a while and see what shows up," I said.

Standing back-to-back we could glass everything below and to the three sides. From this crag we could see almost three quarters of the big open meadow called Sheep Flats. This meadow was immediately above and bordered the north side of Churn Creek. It was reasonably level toward the mountain and about 1,200 yards wide. This grassy plateau would be more than 400 acres. We counted some 35 deer moving about as they grazed in small bunches.

"The sheep have already moved to higher ground;" I told Gary.

"Yeah, but look at those big hatracks down there! I'd be glad to settle for any one of them as a trophy."

"Don't forget, we are hunting sheep today," I reminded him with a laugh. "Start glassing the timber and forget about those big bucks."

"I can see five sheep about half a mile down and to our left," Gary whispered excitedly some minutes later.

"Any rams?" I asked.

"Can't tell. Better have a look."

Focusing for the longer distance, I was able to make out a movement, the five animals moving through trees. They were about 1,000 feet below and would soon come into the open. If they kept travelling we would soon get a good look.

"Check your rifle and get down where you'll have a rest. If there is a ram in that bunch it's going to be one hell of a long shot. Get a sandwich out of your lunch and we'll each eat a half. It helps to stave off the shakes. I'm starting to feel a bit jittery," I said.

We had taken a couple of bites when two sheep broke out of the timber onto the open slope. Dropping what was left of our sandwiches, we put up the binocs. The two were a few yards apart and walking away from the sun. They stopped to look in every direction frequently.

"Mother and her lamb," Gary said softly.

"Yeah! Keep watching," I whispered, as a third sheep trotted out.

"Another ewe!" he said with disappointment. The three sheep moved ahead another 100 yards and stopped. They turned their heads to stare back along their trail. We could hear the rattling of rolling rocks. Then two darker and larger sheep charged along the trail and came to a halt behind the last ewe.

"My God! They're rams!" Gary exclaimed.

All five turned their heads, staring in our direction and stood motionless.

"Have to take them now, so listen carefully," I ordered quietly. "Move slowly. When you have your scope on the one closest to the last ewe, let me know. I'll take the back one when you are ready. Count 1-2-3. We fire at the start of three."

I could hear his breathing increase and knew he was having a real problem keeping his cool. Sheep fever.

My rifle was lined well under the chest of the second ram. At three both rifles roared. I swear mountain sheep can go from stop to 50 miles an hour in a single bound and maintain that speed until out of sight. The four front animals became a blur of gray, charging toward the next canyon. The last ram wheeled sideways, staggered, then bounded down across the rock slide and disappeared.

Gary had fired twice more. I could see his bullets kick up puffs of dust and snow, a good 10 feet above his sheep's back. Shooting downhill, that's how much a 130-grain 270 bullet rises in 500 yards.

"Missed him clean! Forgot to allow for downhill," he said disgustedly.

"I'm pretty sure I hit the back one but at that distance it's hard to know. Let's head down and have a look."

We were halfway there when we heard shooting. Seven quick rifle shots about a mile to our left and above.

"That will be Tom and Syro. Our shots must have spooked another ram in their direction. Hope they did better."

We came to the spot where the trail left the timber edge. There was a small open meadow. Fresh snow was two inches deep. It was like reading a book in sheep tracks. While the ewes had walked straight through, the two rams had squared off for battle. They had backed off until they were 50 to 60 feet apart, then charged. The tracks showed this happened three times. One had been knocked off his feet. We figured this knockdown happened on the last charge.

"Their rutting season is just about over. One of those ewes is the reason for the fight," I explained.

"This is why the first three stopped to look back," Gary said. "Funny we didn't hear them banging away at each other."

"One thing is for sure. We can't cook tracks so we best be moving along."

Where the sheep had stood when we shot there was some hair and a lot of blood where the ram had taken off down the mountain.

"This one can't go far bleeding like that. Looks like you had a clean miss on the other one, Gary."

"Think I should trail the bugger and try for another shot?"

"No use. I tried two years ago to follow across that steep slope and got stuck. It took me almost an hour to dig toe-holds so I could back up. It was too steep to go ahead or to turn around so I just backed up. It's too dangerous when it's dry. With this much snow it's suicide."

"Hate to be so close and have him get away," Gary argued.

"Best you could hope for if you try to follow is some broken bones at the bottom of the canyon. Let's go after my ram."

It was easy to follow the tracks and blood. Half a mile farther down the rocky slope we spotted our prize at the bottom of a canyon. Stone dead. After dressing him out we figured he'd weigh more than 150 pounds. The bullet had severed one of the arteries from the heart.

"You know, Joe, it's hard to believe any animal hit that way could travel so far. A deer would have dropped dead on the spot."

"These bighorn rams can't be compared to any other animal. Bill Auchinachie swears that they are crossed with some sort of a steel spring."

"How are we going to get him out?" Gary asked with concern, looking at the steep walls of the canyon.

"It's eleven o'clock and I'm about starved," he declared.

"There's good water in that little creek so we might as well eat before we start packing," I suggested.

When we had finished lunch my nephew looked away for several minutes, and said thoughtfully, "Why do you suppose Ted and Don forgot to meet us yesterday morning?"

It was evident this had been bothering him.

I walked over and picked up the full curl ram's head, held it out, one hand on each horn so it was facing straight at him.

"This is the reason. Take a good look," I said. "They spotted this fellow yesterday morning. If that isn't reason enough to make a man forget almost everything else, then I don't know what is."

"Yeah! I get the picture better now that we are here and all this has happened," Gary said quietly.

"Here, take the head up to our gear. There's a coil of rope in the back of my coat. Throw one end down to me and we will heave this baby up to where we can pack it. The real work starts now!"

We made our way up to the rim, taking turns at packing the head and the carcass. We reached the Jeep in five hours. We had climbed about 3,000 feet and covered eight miles. It was dusk by the time our trophy was hanging on the meat pole back at camp.

Tom and Ted had also scored. Johnny and Brad had missed two whopper rams three miles from camp. Don, Gordon, and Bill had each brought in a good buck. The order of the hour was hot rums.

Syro had already nicknamed the General "Ike."

"Can't remember Jimmy Watt," he said, "so from now on you are just plain 'Ike.' He was a five star so I've given you a promotion."

"Suits me and you don't even have to salute those extra stars."

Everyone chuckled. Happy times. A good day, and Jimmy was 'Ike' for the rest of the trip.

Bill had brought in a young buck for camp meat. Bert had built up the stew and cut enough steaks to last a week.

"All we need now is a couple of blue grouse for extra flavour. Saw some right near camp. That's my job for tomorrow," Bert told us as he poked the fire.

Supper and all the chores were finished by about seven. We were just sitting around swapping yarns and we got chatting about wolves and coyotes. We could hear them howling from our camp. Lots of them. There was a "Yip, Yip, Ooooooo," from the woods close by.

"Our uninvited guest," Bert laughed. "He came out and watched me for half an hour this morning. Young. About half grown."

"I'm wondering if you had any experience with rabid wolves and coyotes while you were stationed up in the Northwest Territories," Tom said to Gary.

"I flew all through that country around Great Slave Lake

in summer of '50. We landed at Hay River, went on to Yellowknife, then up the Mackenzie River as far as Fort Simpson. The police warned us not to go anywhere without a gun. They said the wolves have rabies. A bite is fatal. Gotta be careful."

"Yeah," Gary replied, "I was right in the middle of it. For several months two of us were out with a closed-in jeep, two sawed-off shotguns, automatic pistols, a rifle apiece and hundreds of rounds of ammo.

"First we had to be inoculated. That was a God-awful thing. The doctor gives you the shot in the gut. The needle looked six inches long. Then we had to be under observation for nine days. We studied up on how the disease spread and what to do if someone was bitten. The inoculation is really a mild case of the disease itself. By the fourth day I had a temperature over 103, stomach pains and a blinding headache. The doctor said we would probably survive a bite from an infected animal, but we'd have to get to a doctor damn quick if it happened. Rabies is passed on from one animal to another mostly by a bite. The bitten one goes mad. It gets worse fast and will attack anything that moves. By the seventh and eighth day the legs and rear sections are wobbly. Almost paralyzed. The disease affects the brain first and then the whole central nervous system. Most animals die about the ninth day. Wolves, coyotes, foxes are supposed to be the main carriers. Not so. We had bobcats and lynx more than once jump on the hood of our Jeep and try to get at us through the windshield. One tore both wiper blades off. We were too slow turning the 'off' button.

"With time we could tell by the way an animal moved just about what it could do and how advanced the disease was. When they became sleepy and appeared friendly that was the most dangerous time. If anything came close they struck like a rattlesnake.

"When we tired of using our guns, we tied a heavy sack to each wheel, then drove along the frozen roads. The crazed animals would rush in and clamp onto these flying sacks. Dozens died with a broken neck or a smashed head. Once they got a hold, there was no letting go. Sometimes we would have to cut part of the sack away to get them free."

"What about rabbits?" asked Syro.

"They would just stagger around until they fell over and died."

"If something ate the dead animal would they go mad?" asked Don.

"We thought they did but I'm not sure. We shot several bobcats and foxes feeding off these carcasses. This epidemic of rabies was moving steadily south. The big scare at the time was for the safety of children. People were afraid the disease would spread to their house pets.

"Some infected wolves had been killed as far south as Grand Prairie in Alberta. In B.C. there was a real problem around Fort Nelson. A trapper caught several foxes and a coyote north of Dawson Creek, just inside the Alberta border on the Peace River. They were definitely infected. This was considered serious enough to start a poisoning program. Bush planes with pilots who knew that country were hired. Meat baits loaded with 10-80 or arsenic were dropped on the ice of lakes and along most of the rivers."

"What happened to those poison baits if they weren't eaten?" asked Tom.

"They went out with the ice when spring breakup came. When that winter ended so did most of the rabies," Gary replied.

"Did you find any cougar in that north country that had rabies?" asked Tom.

"We didn't see or hear of any. I believe it's too cold for their liking. I've never even seen any tracks in that part of the country," Gary said.

58

Tom got up from the log, walked over and poked the fire until it blazed. He stood with his back to the fire, looked up and tapped his chest.

"You fellows are looking at the only man in the world who has shot a wild cougar off a deer's back," he bragged.

There was silence as we looked at each other then back at Tom until Johnny Ames said, "Tell us about it."

"Jack Sweeney, Joe and me were hunting deer in the big timber up on Mount Sicker late in the fall of '28. It was pouring down rain and I was hunting into a southwest wind. Under the big trees it was like a park. I could hunt without making a sound. Coming out from some trees I spotted a three-point buck standing not more than 75 yards away. He was behind an old log with only part of his back and his neck and head showing. He was looking the opposite way so I took my time.

"I raised the gun and then I saw a flash of brown. I saw the cougar land on the deer's back and the deer's head snapped around. Looking right at me.

"I saw one big front paw hooked onto the buck's nose and the cat opened its mouth wide to bite into the deer's neck. Just below its ear. The near front leg was down over the deer's back holding onto the shoulder. Happened without a sound, in less than five seconds.

"That deer made no attempt to run and it didn't try to struggle, to get free. The two animals just began to settle slowly toward the ground. By the time I'd figured out what to do, there was only about four inches of the cougar's back showing above the top of the log. I sighted the 30.30 on this narrow target and I fired.

"I waited for a minute. Something had to happen. No, just silence. Walking over with the gun at ready I found the cougar was stone dead. Lying there on top of the deer. Grabbed it by that long tail. Pulled it to one side. The buck

59

scared hell out of me when it scrambled to its feet and charged down the hill. I could see the bullet had broken the cougar's back. It died instantly.

"Jack and Joe had heard the shot and were looking for me. They answered my first whistle. Together we dragged the cougar down to the road. Took it straight to Holmans and asked Albert if he would skin it out so the hide and head could be made into a rug.

"Next day we went to see if we could find the deer. Albert had told us he believed the buck would be dead. We followed down a trail for about 200 yards and there was the deer. Dead, cold and bloated. The cougar had bitten through the jugular along the side of its neck. It had bled to death as it tried to run away.

"Joe had a measuring tape. From where the cougar's back claws had torn the bark of the log when it sprang to where it landed on the deer's back was 27 feet."

"How big was the deer?" asked Don.

"Over 125 pounds."

"The cougar. How big?" Ted asked.

"Weighed just over 80 pounds and measured seven feet, tip to tip."

"You got to be a celebrity, Tom," Ike called as he headed for his tent.

"Naw, I was just on the spot."

It took us until noon next day to bring in the two rams that Tom and Ted had packed only part way out. Then we began deer hunting. Does and fawns were everywhere. It was just a matter of time to pick out a big buck and drag it out to a place where it could be loaded. Syro and 'Ike' became real buddies and hunted as a team. They bagged two trophies.

On the seventh day the temperature dropped well below zero so we packed our gear, loaded and headed home. We had to build a fire under the Jeep to get it started.

Eating lunch on the ferry on the way to Vancouver Island, Don did a bit of bookkeeping, "Give me $1.35 each and we're all squared away."

As we fumbled for the change Don picked a parcel from the floor. He handed it over, saying, "You have to open this right here and now or it goes back to Chilliwack."

Gary ripped off the paper. A pair of brand-new oxfords, with socks tucked in.

Jim Dewar and His Hounds

Jim Dewar was indeed a man of the outdoors. He believed if cougars and wolves were kept under control then the deer and other game would be around in healthy numbers. Jim was the first full time predator hunter in British Columbia and later became a full-fledged game warden with the title of Senior Conservation Officer.

Bill Roper was the mine boss in Extension near Nanaimo where Jim worked. His eldest daughter Margaret became fascinated with this rough-and-ready young woodsman. Jim Dewar wasn't the type to run away from any romance. There was a wedding the spring of '28.

The coal mines round about were closing one after another when the stock market crashed in 1929. Jim and Margaret moved to Youbou. There was work in the mill at Lake Cowichan and one of the bosses just happened to be Jim's brother-in-law. Jobs were so scarce that you had to know someone. Jim started on the green chain at 30¢. The young couple rented a little house built on a log float below the sawmill. I first met Jim and his hounds, Patsy and Blue, there. I was sparking Margaret's younger sister Claire at the time.

We had been invited up to see his new cougar hounds. Two blueticks. The first on Vancouver Island. He had purchased them from the Lee brothers in Paradise, Arizona. The Lees were big game guides and probably the best known cougar hunters in North America.

"Let's try them out," I said when I saw them.

We changed boots, gulped a beer with a sandwich and drove as far up the Cottonwood Valley as the Oakland roadster would take us. He handed me Patsy's chain. Blue, almost grown, was not yet fully trained. He nosed ahead and about a mile up the creek tracked and treed a raccoon.

Jim walked to the nearest willow bush and cut a switch. Blue got a good thrashing. He was on leash for the rest of the afternoon.

"Got to break him off deer and coons if he's going to be any good to us in this country," declared the new boss.

A month later there was an early snow, four inches at the mill yard and twice as much halfway up the Cottonwood Valley. We left at daybreak with both hounds. Jim took the lead with Blue on leash and willow switch in hand. Deer and raccoon tracks were everywhere. That young hound never once put his nose down. Two miles farther at the end of the old railway grade we stopped for a breather.

"I'm going to let Blue off his leash. He hasn't shown the slightest interest in the deer or coon tracks."

"How did you manage to break him in such a short time?" I asked.

Jim flexed the switch between his hands and rubbed along the young dog's back.

"A sharp crack over the nose at exactly the right moment has done the trick." He told me how he had worked his dogs for two hours every day since our last hunt. "Already they've treed three cougar. With the bounty money and what I get for the hides there should be enough to pay for the dog feed and leave a bit for other things."

The hounds were sniffing the breeze off the west slope. Patsy let out strange whimpers and Jim started up the hillside. Both dogs moved out, heads high. Sure enough, 200 yards ahead in a shallow gully we came on the carcass of a fresh-killed yearling doe. There was blood and plenty of cougar tracks. The killer's trail went up the slope to the northwest. The dogs soon were charging up the hill bellowing their lungs out.

The chase put the cougar well to the north before it circled back to the southeast. It kept to the timber at the top of the ridge. Breaking into a run I soon got up to where all the excitement was. Jim was already there, looking up into the thick branches of a hemlock. About 50 feet up we spotted the head and shoulders of the big cat. Its ears were back and its eyes followed every movement of the excited hounds.

"Want me to shoot it?" I blurted out excitedly.

"Not yet," Jim ordered. "We can let the dogs have their fun while we look things over. Not much chance of it bailing out from that height. Lend me your binoculars for a minute." He glassed the big cat. "Fully-grown female. Due to have a batch of kittens any day now."

"Let's leave the old girl up there. She's not likely to leave this area before the kittens are born. I'll probably have her up a tree three or four more times before we collect the bounties."

We put both hounds on leash and headed for the car. Halfway down the sidehill a nice buck jumped out from some logs. He bounded to the top of a low ridge, then stood to look back.

"Shall I take him?" I asked, as my thumb pulled the hammer back on the 32-Special.

Dale and Cllel Lee, about 1930. Taken near Paradise, Arizona, U.S.A. Buck is the hound near cougar's head. The other hound near Cllel is Blue. Blue is one of the first cougar hounds Jim Dewar brought to Vancouver Island. The cougar measured over nine feet and weighed almost 200 pounds. The Lee brothers were considered the best and most experienced cougar hunters of their time.   COURTESY: MRS. DEWAR

Jim Dewar with one of his young hounds at Extension, near Nanaimo, British Columbia.
COURTESY: MRS. JIM DEWAR

Cougar shot near Youbou, Cowichan Lake, B.C., August 1934. Hounds are Patsy and Blue. Cougar measured nine feet. Float houses belong to the sawmill company and are rented by the Dewars and the Caldwells who trap and hunt cougar. COURTESY: MRS. DEWAR

Frank Weir and Jim Dewar, 1936, admiring a couple of their hounds. COURTESY: MRS. JIM DEWAR

Mt. Whymper search party. *Standing left to right*; Jim Dewar, Pete Maffeo, Cpl. Hailes. *Sitting*; Bert Tannock, Lt. Cherry Lee and Frank Greenfield.

This was the search party organized to locate the R.C.A.F. bomber that crashed on Mt. Whymper, spring 1944, five killed. Wreckage found noon June 3, 1944. Plane and crew blown to smithereens and scattered for half a mile. The horse is one of a number of the army horses that were used to help with the salvage of the five-ton gondola and other heavy equipment.

COURTESY: MRS. DEWAR

Mt. Whymper, June 12, 1944, Airship K83. Huge air bag resting on top of its gondola. Men are taking out instruments in preparation for loading gondola on a log sleigh. The gondola was winched out some 15 miles to a waiting truck. Air bag was left where it crashed.

Gondola of 245-foot Airship K83 on its way out to the nearest road. It's out of the worst terrain and down into some fairly easy going. Jim Dewar supervised this operation. This part of the ship was loaded on an American destroyer in Nanaimo Harbour and taken back to California to be repaired.

COURTESY: FRANK GREENFIELD

Pete Maffeo with cougar kittens. He and Jim Dewar found them in a den back out in the Nanaimo Lakes area. Note: you can see the rings beginning to fade on the tail of the one in the middle. COURTESY: MRS. DEWAR

Gamewardens Frank Greenfield and Jim Dewar,
1947. They shot the five cougars on a six-day hunt
in the Nanaimo Lakes area.   COURTESY: MRS. DEWAR

June 1949, Jim Dewar on his way to the west coast to take care of a
problem cougar.   COURTESY: MRS. DEWAR

Extension, B.C., January 28, 1949. Mr. and Mrs. Tom Dewar. Their son Jim with cougar and hounds in the centre. Note the slagpile from one of the old coal mines in the background.   COURTESY: MRS. JIM DEWAR

Jim with Scot and Scout, picture taken by Mrs. Boothwick in 1952 at Kyuquot. Scot (left) was killed by a cougar on Read Island a week later.

Tom Dewar (Jim's dad), August 1952. Taken at their home in Extension some six miles southwest of Nanaimo. Cougar and half grown wolf captured near headwaters of Nanaimo River. Wolf had to be put away when he became belligerent.   COURTESY: MRS. DEWAR

Tom Dewar feeding a couple of wild deer he had made friends with near his home in Extension. Jim had shot the cougar that morning when it killed a deer just up behind his house. The two in the picture don't seem to have any great fear of the dead cougar.   COURTESY: MRS. DEWAR

Bill Watt, 1980, with one of the largest cougars ever killed in this province. It was shot near Barriere, north of Kamloops Lake in the interior. Bill tracked this old tom for a week. It had killed and eaten several cougar kittens. He finally caught up with the beast eating on a freshly killed moose. It weighed over 170 pounds and measured 9 feet 2 inches, tip to tip.

"No!" snapped Jim. "Shooting a deer so soon after chasing the cougar could confuse these hounds for the rest of their lives. We can take the dogs home and get a deer later. There's plenty down by the lake. Not as far to pack either."

We led his hounds right over the spot where the deer had stood. They showed no interest. Jim petted both dogs with pride.

"These two will probably be the finest cougar dogs this province has ever seen," he predicted.

That afternoon I met Charlie Caldwell and his wife in their float house next to the Dewars. Both families made good home brew. Mrs. Caldwell's was rated the best in the community. We had emptied several bottles when Charlie announced that he had a story to tell. He signalled his wife for fresh beer, then sat upright in his easy chair. He was ready for action.

"I've heard you bend the truth a bit sometimes," his wife reminded him.

"Thing only happened last spring," old Charlie protested, "so's it's not likely I could forget. This story is the gospel truth.

"Wolves had been howling across the lake nearly all night. Not being able to sleep I got up about three in the morning and rowed over to investigate. I pulled the rowboat into the channel of that creek that runs out on Ashburnams' beach. It was still more than an hour before daylight so I just waited in the boat and must have dozed off.

"I was awakened by the sound of something shuffling in the sand. By now, it was getting light so I just kept still to look and listen. About 20 feet away, two dark objects were moving about. As it got lighter these two critters began shifting back toward the main lake. They had only about 50 yards to go to the water's edge.

"They looked exactly like two black flat-bottomed rowboats upside down. Each would be between five or six feet long and about four feet wide. The highest part of them would be just under three feet above the ground. They travelled one right behind the other. As they entered the water they sort of bobbed along for about 200 feet, then sank out of sight.

"I watched, for almost half an hour. They didn't surface. I examined their trail and found what looked like flipper marks about the size of a sea lion's. By the imprints in the sand, I would guess their weight to be well above 600 pounds.

"I saw their heads and those beady eyes. I swear they were a couple of huge turtles that were planning to spawn on that beach."

There was silence as old Charlie ended his tale. We wanted to know more about Lake Cowichan's own Ogopogo, the legendary monster.

Charlie told us the old Indian legend of a terrible monster that they believed haunted *Kaatza*, their word for lake. Only white men call it Lake Cowichan.

"The Indians say this monster would attack their canoes and swallow an Indian at a single gulp. If there were several in their big canoes, all would be eaten. Then, suddenly, as if triggered, lightning would flash, thunder roar and the skies turn black with a terrible storm.

"Kaatza is more than 500 feet deep in places. The lake bottom is well below sea level. The legend tells of a passage leading from Kaatza's deepest part out to Nitinat Lake and on into the Pacific. The natives believed that this terrible monster came from the ocean by way of this underwater passage.

"Now remember, this lake never freezes all the way across no matter how cold the winters are. So don't scoff when I say that there has to be warm springs down in those deeper

66

areas. That's why those turtles can continue to live here after millions of years. Sure does make a feller wonder. That's my Ogopogo story."

The Caldwells, with their solid independence, didn't believe in working for wages. They kept a large flock of barred-rock chickens which were fed from the scraps left over at the company cook house. Mrs. Caldwell was a crack shot and used a .38 six-gun to get grouse, venison and even wild duck for a change of diet. Woe betide the raccoon or chicken hawk that molested her hens!

They developed a floating garden on a large raft of small logs. Over the logs they placed a layer of balsam boughs. They towed this raft up to the delta of Cottonwood Creek and with a wheelbarrow loaded on about 10 inches of black loam. The roots of their vegetables had all the moisture needed for fast growth and floating out in the lake as it did the garden was never shaded from the sun. There was a ready market for all their produce even during the Dirty Thirties. Small wonder, since it was the earliest and best garden in Youbou.

Cougar bounties, their garden and the fur Charlie got from his trap line gave them a very satisfying life.

The Caldwells were Jim's idols. "Old Cougar Charlie" taught and encouraged him. When Jim had time away from his job he hunted with Charlie. He was much younger and could keep up with the dogs better, especially in rough country.

In the summer of 1933 shortly before the Dewars left Cowichan Lake to move back to Extension, Jim was on a most unusual cougar hunt. One afternoon he got an urgent call from Carl Swanson who lived at the south end of the North Arm of Cowichan Lake near Sunset Park, a mile south of Youbou.

"Yesus, Yimmie—Bring dogs and gun! Yust see tree cougar on beach!"

Jim arrived with his hounds and was shown fresh tracks. The dogs took the scent and chased the big cats over the top of Bald Mountain and down to the lakeshore on the opposite side. When he caught up to the dogs they were searching along the water's edge. Goat Island is only about a quarter mile to the west. Jim concluded the cougar had taken to the water and swum to get away from the hounds. It was late evening.

He ran the two miles back to his pickup and drove to Youbou. It was dark by the time he had rowed his flat-bottomed skiff, loaded with four dogs, out to Goat Island. With cougars on this small, brushy island it was no place to be alone. The hounds went roaring off and were barking treed in a matter of minutes. Jim caught up to the dogs and his carbide light picked up two pairs of piercing eyes about 40 feet up in an old fir. The dim light showed only the outline of their bodies. The cougars were shot. One was an old female. The other, a young tom, weighed 60 pounds.

Jim was loading them into the boat when he heard the hounds barking again. He made his way toward the noise. Two more pairs of eyes shone, glaring at him, only 40 feet up. Jim finished them with one shot each. He was dragging the pair to the boat when his dim lamp picked up a fifth cougar. It was not 20 feet away. He shot it out of a bushy cedar with his last shell.

It was 2:00 a.m. when he tied the big skiff to the float near his cabin. Jim didn't bother to go to bed. Daylight came before the hounds were fed and the five cougar hung up. He jogged the half mile up to the mill to be at the green chain in time to start another tough day.

The mill was cutting hemlock that week. At the end of this shift he drank a cool bottle of home brew and his wife had to shake him awake to eat supper. Only one cougar had been skinned when he put away his knife and called it a day.

Before crawling into bed he phoned the mill and told them he was quitting and wanted his pay cheque in the morning.

Jim Dewar had made up his mind to live more like the Caldwells. He hadn't slept for 30 hours.

In the mid 1930's the B.C. Game Department named Jim a designated predator hunter. In 1942 he moved to Port Alberni where his duties included those of game warden as well as predator control officer.

On June 19, 1949 Domonic Taylor, a seven-year-old Indian boy, was mauled and killed by a cougar on the beach near the Kyuquot Reserve. This village is between the villages of Ucluelet and Tofino northwest of Port Alberni on Vancouver Island's west coast.

The boy was playing among driftwood only a short distance from his home. The cougar leapt out, smashed him with a paw and dragged the youngster into the heavy salal and underbrush.

The mother ran to the village for help. Someone phoned the police who called Jim Dewar in Port Alberni.

Jim wasted no time. He called Alberni Air Lines to arrange for a float plane and then took his four hounds to the airbase. Skate Hames, another government cougar hunter, went along to give a hand. They were on their way in less than an hour.

Flying to the scene of the tragedy took 70 minutes and another half hour by truck. The hunters took less than 40 minutes to tree this 80-pound male. Dewar finished it with a bullet to the head. In the stomach they found parts of a dog and half of a raccoon. A search in the underbrush turned up the remains of two raccoons and a partly-eaten dog.

"That cougar didn't kill the boy because it was hungry," the constable declared emphatically.

Taylor and his wife wept as their child was carried out to the road. Jim was trying to console the grief-stricken parents.

"Why him kill my boy?" the father asked.

"Him like zootsuiter," Jim answered, pointing to the dead killer. "Him maybe two and half or three years old. Him like some bad young man—go around like crazy, fight all time and destroy anything he don't like."

"I think maybe you right," the father replied.

*   *   *

Recently I discussed the west coast cougar population with Tom MacDonald. He had moved from Extension to the coast in 1952 where he became a registered cougar hunter.

"Let's hear what happened, Tom," I asked.

"Cougars were all around us. The police would call the hunters in from Port Alberni when the big cats were sighted or caused trouble.

"If the school bus wasn't running our two girls had to pedal their bikes 10 miles each way to school in Ucluelet. The old bus was out of commission most of the time. The brush and salal grew so close to the road that there was barely room for single lane traffic. There were other children along this road who had to wait for the bus or ride their bikes. We were always afraid that the cougar would attack from the heavy cover of the salal. A wild and scary position to be in.

"To cap it, one evening my wife Vickie saw two cougar on the road right in front of our house. A call went in and Jimmie Dewar was there next day. Having known Jim from Extension where we grew up together it was only natural that he stayed at our place whenever he was called to the area. This time he stayed for a week. We shot five cougar so close that the wife could hear the hounds barking treed on every one, right from our porch.

"On the fourth day we knew that there were still more cougar around by the way Jim's three dogs were acting. Only one dog was a seasoned hunter. The two younger ones were still learning.

70

"Sure enough, on our first hunt that day his best dog was killed by a cougar only 40 yards off the road. There was no use trying with only the two pups.

"Jim left for Alberni early next morning. Said he would try again to get enough money to buy more hounds. Apparently the department was always short of funds when Jim needed dogs. Remember, now, this was shortly after the little Taylor boy had been killed so naturally the people were jittery about the safety of their families.

"On his next trip, Jim came out on the old *Uchuck*. She was the passenger and freight boat that ran between Alberni and the west coast. He had been able to get some extra dogs, so he left a couple there for me. He figured that it would save the game department hundreds of dollars if I could look after the calls out there. That year they made me a registered hunter. There was a $40 double bounty for every cougar that I shot.

"By 1953 I had enough experience and confidence to handle most of the local calls. There were many and at all hours of the day or night. In June alone that year I shot five not a mile from our house. Logging camps as far away as 20 miles would call me in when they spotted one.

"Two years later Jim got an urgent call from the chief of the Ahousat Indian village, some 40 miles north on Flores Island. This island was right out in the open Pacific Ocean with no land between it and Japan. Jim phoned me to bring three dogs and meet him on the dock at Ucluelet come daylight next morning.

"At dawn when the Beaver aircraft was tied to the dock my dogs were put in the back with the four that were already there. We took off smoothly but got into some wind and considerable turbulence about 20 miles out. This started a vicious dog fight in back. Jim undid his safety belt and scrambled back into that snarling tangle, bare handed. In less than five minutes, he managed to quieten them down. He had a way with dogs that is hard to explain.

"I tell you, the plane did some pretty fancy dips and dives what with all those dogs jumping around. I'm nervous in planes at the best of times, and was wishing to be anywhere else about that time. However it wasn't long until Paul Sam, the chief, was welcoming us at the Ahousat landing. We had been there only two weeks before and shot two big cougar that had been eating their dogs.

"'Where's the man who was attacked?' Jim asked.

"'Take my boat. He's four mile up there cutting more wood,' the chief said, pointing up the bay.

"Jim gave me a strange look as we beached the boat and stepped ashore. We found the man who had persuaded his chief to call us in. He was busy cutting wood at the edge of a clearing. We looked the situation over. If this man had been mauled it certainly didn't show!

"'Where did you see the cougar?'

"'Not see him. Hear noise in bush there,' the Indian answered, pointing toward the edge of the clearing.

"We took two of the best hounds into the timber. They found no scent and trotted back to stand behind us. We covered the area for half a mile or more. There was nothing, no tracks, no scent, only an Indian who, by then, had forgotten how to talk!

"I'd never seen Jim so mad and disgusted.

"'We've come almost 200 miles with seven dogs and a float plane to hunt a noise!' he exploded. 'This trip will probably cost the taxpayers more than $500 for nothing.'

"I looked at my watch. It was not yet eight a.m.

"When we landed back at Ucluelet there was a message waiting. Ray Arthur, the man in charge of the telephone service, had left word that two cougars had just torn down the net fence to get at his chickens. We knew Ray to be a reliable man.

72

"Maybe this damned trip won't be a total loss after all," Jim remarked, a bit more cheerful as we piled the seven dogs into the back of my pickup and headed for the Arthur place.

"Mrs. Arthur showed us the pen and pointed, 'One went in there, and the one with the chicken in its mouth went behind our house.'

"I got my three dogs out first and looked at Jim for direction.

"'Take the one without the chicken first.'

"Things didn't work out quite the way Jim expected. His four dogs took after the one with the chicken. The brush and salal was so thick you couldn't see 20 feet ahead. Meanwhile, in the opposite direction, I could hear mine barking treed not 100 yards away.

"You had to do more crawling than walking to make any headway at all. When I got near enough I could see the big cat up a yew tree, of all places. The tip of its long tail was only about eight feet from the ground and all three dogs were jumping up trying to grab it. It was a skinny mean-looking female. I didn't hesitate. One 30-30 bullet into its head finished the brute! Now I hurried back.

"Jim was waiting at the edge of the clearing. 'This bastard just killed one of my young dogs.' He held a mangled chicken in his hand. 'It left the chicken and carried off the dog. Sure not one of our better days. My other dogs won't go after it. They can smell the dead dog and are afraid.'

"'What do you figure we should try now?'

"Jim looked at the ground for quite a while before answering, 'A cougar gives off an aggressive scent in a case like this. Few dogs will track such an animal. I've been through something similar to this only once before but in more open country. When I put my best hound on a short leash, she would follow the trail. Unless I was right up close she would come back and walk behind me. You carry the gun and be ready to shoot, I'll handle old Bounce. You want to give it a try?'

"'Sure do.'

"Bounce was one of his oldest and most reliable hounds. Jim had given him to me a few months earlier. 'These damn cougar out here are mean,' Jim protested, 'Dogs are part of their regular diet. Here we are hunting them with their favourite food. Not too smart,' he finished with that crooked grin.

"'Think it's safe to try with only one dog in this thick brush?'

"'You stay close with the rifle ready and we'll have a go at it.'

"Old Bounce, now on leash, took the trail, but we could see he was nervous. I stayed close while Jim kept urging him forward. A quarter of a mile down the trail we came on the dead dog. It was lying in the centre of a small open area, near a spruce tree. The cougar had raked all the hair from the rib cage, torn off the flesh and eaten the heart, liver and lungs. Every drop of blood had been licked from inside the body cavity.

"Old Bounce sniffed his dead buddy, did some whimpering, then backed off to stand behind Jim. No amount of urging made the slightest difference. Bounce was not going to follow the trail any farther.

"'That trap that I gave you. Is it at your house now?'

"'Sure is,' I said.

"'You leave me the gun,' he directed. 'Take old Bounce to the truck, then go get the trap and some wire. I'll keep watch while you're gone.'

"It took me more than half an hour to find the big trap and get back to Jim. He was hunkered down by his dead dog.

"'Feel this dog's head if you want to know the power of a cougar's front feet.'

74

"The skull was shattered. I pressed my fingers where the big claw marks showed above the dog's eyes. It was like feeling a sack of peas.

"We wired the dog's body to the tree, set the trap right in front, then covered it with twigs. When we came back next morning, we had a 90-pound tom cougar caught by a front foot! We carried him to the truck in time for Jim to get the boat back home.

"Neither of us suspected that there might be another cougar around. We were both wrong. Next morning when I went in to pick up the trap the dog had been torn off the tree and carried away.

"I hunted the area with four dogs the following morning. The result was a disaster. This vicious old female would not tree. She turned, fought and killed another dog. I quit the hunt and went home.

"When the game department cut off all cougar bounties in 1957 I was forced to give my dogs away. I could no longer afford to feed them. That was the end of my cougar hunting.

"You know, I was talking to Dan Lay a few days ago. He is now the predator hunter for Vancouver Island, and doing a real fine job of it. I told him about the trap incident and the one that got away.

"'I won't hunt those west coast cats with less than six dogs,' Dan told me. 'They are by far the most vicious cougars in all of B.C. The offspring from the female you chased are probably still around being taught by their mothers just how to kill and eat dogs.'"

*　　*　　*

Some years later six of us fought our way miles back along an old railway grade almost to the headwaters of the Chemainus River. We had two pickup trucks, a big tent and lots of beer and cooking equipment. Don Butt, Ted Robson,

75

George Syrotuck, Bill Auchinachie, my brother Tom, and myself left Duncan on a Friday morning, the day before the grouse and deer season was to open. It took us the rest of the day to travel some 12 miles over the old grade. We forded creeks, cut logs and even had to build a crude bridge over one creek where the road had washed away. About eight miles from camp we rolled a huge log across the grade. We didn't want anyone to follow and spoil the privacy. About an hour before dark, the camp was set up.

We nailed up a target to be sure our rifle sights were okay after all that bouncing. More than a dozen shots were fired before we had finished. Robson, picking up his 20-gauge, casually remarked, "Going along the grade to exercise old Pete before I tie him for the night."

He was back in less than half an hour with a dozen young blue grouse, saying "That's breakfast," spilling the birds onto the plywood table.

George Syrotuck did the cleaning and invited me to help. We carried the lot well down into some tall fireweed. We sat on an old log and skinned, cleaned and cut the birds into pan-sized pieces. We put them into two large bowls at the back of the tent, covered them with wine vinegar, added salt and pepper, then pressed them down by a tin plate. Each was weighted with a fair-sized rock.

It was past 11 o'clock. We were playing poker by the light of two gas lanterns when Don Butt decided the grouse best be put out of sight, saying "That was a lot of shooting for the day before the season opens. A game warden could hear that noise for miles."

"It's darker than the inside of a coal mine out there," Ted argued. "There's no game warden going to walk that trail at this time of night."

"I'm going to put them out of sight anyway," Don said and he and George picked up the bowls and went to the truck.

76

The poker game resumed after they returned and each of us had a fresh beer. Ted and I were at the back end of the table. We hadn't finished the beer when Ted nudged me with an elbow and whispered, "Look!" The flaps of the tent parted and there stood Jim Dewar! The game warden.

His eyes searched everywhere in our tent before he spoke, "I'm a game warden. Heard the shooting. Where's the grouse?"

"Just making sure our guns were okay on some targets," Don explained.

"Didn't sound like target practice to me. I'm going to search your camp," Jim announced and he looked into sleeping bags, pots, pans, every place that might hide a grouse. He even opened some of the beer cartons in Don's truck. Half an hour had passed since he had arrived. As Jim was opening another box of beer Don suggested he have one with us, join the poker game and be a bit more friendly.

"Got an extra sleeping bag in my truck if you want to spend what's left of the night here," I suggested. "Where's your vehicle?"

"Couldn't roll that log off the grade so I walked from there. No, I'll be taking off now. Nothing for me here."

"Would you like to borrow one of the lanterns?" Ted asked.

"Don't need any light to travel in this kind of weather," and he left as quietly as he had arrived.

"How come you were so generous with the beer?" I asked Don.

"Thought something should be done and quick," Don answered, "because the grouse were hidden in that beer case Jim was starting to open," and he gave a tense little giggle. Shooting out of season was a very serious offence.

Two years later Tom, George Syrotuck and I stopped for a routine game check near Duncan. As Jim examined our licences, he casually asked if we remembered the tent episode.

"Sure do," Tom answered.

Jim surprised us with this request asking, "Now that it's all over, will you tell me exactly where the grouse were hidden when I checked your camp?"

"You go ahead and tell him the truth," Tom suggested to George, laughing.

"You had your hand on the beer box the grouse were in when Don suggested you join us for a drink," George confessed.

"I'll be damned," Jim remarked quietly.

*   *   *

On Friday, May 26, 1944, a Royal Canadian Air Force bomber with its crew of five men crashed on Mount Whymper. This rugged mountain, 4,600 feet high, is some 20 miles southwest of Nanaimo.

The crash was first reported from the Mount Brenton forestry lookout. The fire watcher had heard a blast and seen a plume of black smoke some 20 miles to the northwest.

Pete Maffeo was head of the local civil defence so the provincial police told him to take charge of the search and rescue. He first called Frank Greenfield, the senior game warden in Nanaimo. Next he contacted Flight Lieutenant Lee, of the R.C.A.F. sea plane base at Patricia Bay near Sidney, near Victoria. A Canso was immediately put at his disposal. At six a.m. the next day the two game wardens, Frank Greenfield and Jim Dewar, along with Bert Tannock of the Royal Canadian Mounted Police, boarded the flying boat in Ladysmith Harbour. They searched all that day and well into the next before spotting some bits of clothing hanging in the trees near the top of Mount Whimper.

The airplane, fully loaded with bombs, had exploded on impact. Pieces of plane and people were scattered for half a mile. Jim Dewar described it as being "blown to matchwood."

A ground crew of six men was organized and they started in from Jump Lake at daylight, Monday, May 29. Pete Maffeo had devised an unusual scheme to save time and get a message out from the search party. Tom Naylor of Nanaimo had carrier pigeons. Maffeo asked him to lend four of his best birds. Pop Dorman worked all night to finish a cage for the rough trip.

When Dewar saw this box on top of all the rest of the gear they would have to carry on their backs, he went to Pete and Tom to protest.

"Think those noisy birds can find their way out of all that timber?"

"Just put your message in the container, but be sure it's properly fastened to the pigeon's leg. Turn the bird loose and I'll guarantee we will have your message in less than an hour," Tom Naylor explained indignantly.

The search in this rough area took these experienced woodsmen until Saturday, June 3, to locate what was left of the bomber and its crew. Two of the pigeons were released carrying this information.

This headline appeared in *The Nanaimo Daily Free Press*, Monday, June 5, 1944:

FOUR FLIERS MAY BE LOST IN THE HILLS
LOCAL SEARCHERS RETURN FROM MOUNT WHYMPER

FOUND REMAINS OF ONLY ONE AIRMAN

Some of the searchers staying at the wreck to look for other members of the bomber crew.

On June 5, the last two pigeons were released. Headlines

in *The Nanaimo Daily Free Press* Tuesday, June 6, 1944, the next day, follow:

U.S. "MERCY BLIMP" IS WRECKED NEAR NANAIMO ELEVEN ABOARD COME DOWN WITH NOT A SCRATCH!

245 FOOT GASBAG IS DRAWN DOWNWARD IN CANYON; NOW HANGS IN TREETOPS

Circling winds had dashed the blimp against the canyon sides, ripping holes in her fabric.

Six of this crew walked out while five remained to guard the instruments and aid in the search for the missing bomber crewmen.

The Nanaimo Daily Free Press reported:

After examination of the wreckage, it is believed none of the air crew had bailed out. A party which started in over the tortuous trail leading from Jump Creek above the Waterworks Dam into the Mount Whymper area contains a Protestant Minister and a Catholic padre whose duty it is to conduct forest burial services for victims of the plane crash. This party, according to the two-watt walkie-talkie being used, is "stalled" partway and unable to proceed further.

In this rough terrain a walkie-talkie would be useful for no more than five miles. The request for the priest and padre came in with the last two carrier pigeons.

In a discussion with Jim Dewar in the fall of 1948, he told me what he remembered of the ordeal.

"It was the toughest month I ever spent in the woods. The 20-mile hike in wasn't too bad. When we found the wreckage of the bomber and started to look for the crew, it was sickening.

80

"At first, we thought some had bailed out before the crash. On the second day, we were finding the bones and clothing of several different men. Ten days of hot weather had done terrible things to the remains of the bomber crew. Flies, maggots, ravens and buzzards had carried off or eaten a good portion of what was left. An air force doctor came in and tried to put the pieces of bones together to make up five different bodies. He gave up the second day. There were too many pieces missing.

"The smell was so bad that no one on the crew ever kept breakfast down for more than an hour. The largest piece we found was a flying boot with the foot still in it. The stripped leg bones stuck up out of the boot almost to where the knee had been. The next largest was part of a hip and pelvis with some underwear still on it.

"The doctor decided there were parts of five different men. He also thought it would be better to bury the remains out in the woods.

"The Catholic priest was in no shape to make the last steep climb. Four of us used a couple of stretchers. We loaded the bits and pieces we had found and carried them down to the clergymen. Here in among some big fir trees, the burial and service took place. We made a rough wooden cross and put it at the end of the grave to mark the spot. Someone carved the five names on it the following day.

"Next, we helped the American marines, who had crashed in the blimp, pack out some heavy radar equipment they had taken out of the airship. This was taken into Nanaimo and locked in the main vault of the bank. Guards were posted to protect these top secret radar gadgets 24 hours a day.

"We had a meeting that night at police headquarters. We had top brass from the army camp in Harewood, Pete Maffeo and several of his men from civil defence plus some top air force officers from Vancouver. Then there was

Captain Howard Coulter, head of the Pacific fleet of air ships for the U.S.A.

"Coulter was the one who was so anxious to try and salvage the airship. He talked mostly to Greenfield and myself. He guaranteed us all the men we needed plus equipment and the money for wages and other expenses.

"'Give us until ten o'clock tomorrow and we will let you know,' I promised him.

"Frank and I spent what was left of the night phoning loggers, contractors, and some equipment men. We had our boss, Frank Butler, out of bed before six next morning to see if he would give us a leave of absence for a month. When we explained what it was for, the answer was a big "Yes." We were promised help from the loggers, the army and the forestry department.

"At 10 o'clock, we met with Captain Coulter and told him of our plan. First of all, the big damaged airbag we would leave where it was. Second, we would build a big log sleigh at the site, then load the gondola and all the equipment aboard the sleigh. That done, a road or right-of-way would be slashed out. The sleigh carrying the gondola would be winched out to the nearest truck road.

"Captain Coulter wanted to know how long it would take.

"'Three weeks if we're lucky, four if we're not,' I told him.

"'Go ahead and do it. Our navy will look after the costs.'

"We shook hands.

"Falling all those trees for the road was the back-breaker. Two shifts went 18 hours a day. Everything was cut low. No stump over 12 inches above the ground. We had men from the army with powder to knock out any high rock and blow the big logs off the road.

"With the help of some horses and a couple of army winches, we were ready to load the gondola on a big flatdeck truck 21 days later.

"The American navy had a destroyer waiting at the dock in Nanaimo to take the equipment back to California. That's about all there was to it.

"I remember being very tired and glad the job was over. It was only because we knew that backwood country between Nanaimo Lakes and Cowichan Lake better than anyone else that we were asked to do the job."

In the spring of 1984 I went to visit Frank Greenfield to find out what he remembered about the crash.

Frank is in his 80's now. He and his wife live in Nanaimo in their home overlooking Departure Bay. His mind is sharp and he still has the stride of a woodsman.

I showed him some pictures of the airship hanging in the trees that Mrs. Jim Dewar had loaned me. He then read the write-up from *The Nanaimo Daily Free Press*. His reaction to the article was sharp.

"Damn paper didn't know the facts. Because the radar equipment was all hush-hush at the time we couldn't tell them anything about it. Papers didn't even know we had the most important radar parts locked up in the bank. They didn't even know the American navy was guarding this because the men were all in civilian clothes.

"We couldn't tell them about the six 500-pound depth charges the airship had dropped when it tried to get some altitude just before it crashed. Couldn't tell them there were only two ships like the K83 equipped with radar on the Pacific coast. If they had known they still couldn't have printed all this. There was still the threat of enemy invasion along the Pacific coast.

"A bomb expert had been sent from England to set off the depth charges. We were afraid a forest fire would result if we did this before the fall rains set in. Bill was his first name. I can't remember his last. Anyway, we hiked in and looked things over."

"'I'll need a mile of wire,' he told me.

"Jim Dewar was plenty husky in those days so in September I got him to help us pack the wire and other gadgets to the depth charges.

"Bill must have lost 10 pounds in sweat while he was connecting the six charges together. When I asked him if he was scared, he answered this way, 'Four years ago, when I started this type of work, there were 90 men in my outfit. Now there are only three of us left. I'm not really scared. Just a bit nervous.'

"When he was satisfied everything was ready, we connected the spool of wire and strung it out right up over the top of the hill to the north. Jim carried the plunger. He picked a huge fir about 200 yards down the other side to stand behind.

"When the wires were connected to the battery he warned us to stand tight to the tree. Then he pushed the plunger down. There was a noise like a clap of thunder when it's real close.

"The concussion almost knocked us off our feet. We could hear rocks rolling down the steep walls of the canyon a mile away. We walked back to find all charges gone. It looked like a big truck had dumped a load of gravel where each bomb had lain. One had cut a six-foot fir tree off level with the ground. The job was completed and our friend Bill was on his way back to England the next day.

"The job was finally over. We could never have completed the work without Jim Dewar's knowledge of the area and his skill as a woodsman. Pete Maffeo was a real help, too."

"Have you kept any souvenirs of the wreck?" I asked. Frank went to the basement and brought up a small, white, four-legged stool.

"That's the pilot's seat from the gondola."

He held up a grayish-brown packsack, "And that's made

from the skin of the K83. Almost every logger in this part of the country has a bag like this. They are waterproof, light and very strong."

After the search and salvage work had been completed, Jim Dewar headed back to his home in Port Alberni.

He was glad to get back to his regular game warden duties, cougar hunting and all. His hounds were eager for some exercise. They hadn't had a workout for over a month.

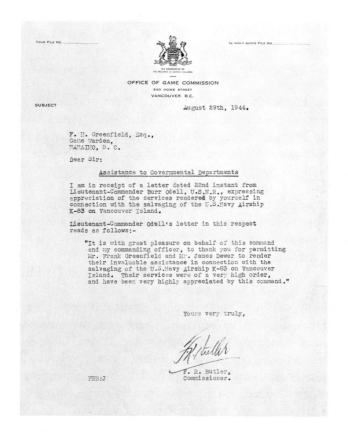

The Holmans Bring'em Back Alive

Grace Elizabeth Richards' parents were among the first pioneers of the Cowichan District. She was born near Maple Bay in February 1885, and married Albert Holman in 1901. The young couple moved to Mount Sicker where Albert had a job in the mine.

Towering to the south of the Chemainus River, this heavily-timbered mountain teemed with wildlife. The copper deposits were rich and rated as the largest in the Pacific Northwest.

"Looks like a good place to start our married life," the young bride said to her mother. "With you and Dad living close by it won't be so lonely for us."

The mine town, perched on a flat 2,700 feet above sea level, housed some 400 miners. There were two hotels with bars and dancing girls. A livery stable, several large bunkhouses, a huge cookhouse, a general store, a school and a post office made up the main part of the business section. Set apart in a wooded area there were some 60 small cottages and a church. This area was for married couples.

In 1903, Albert and Grace had their first baby, Evelyn. Because there was no doctor closer than 10 miles, Mrs. Richards came over to deliver the child. Albert was kept busy looking after the hot water and towels.

Albert and a brother-in-law, Pete Boudot, had both applied for land near the Chemainus River. They were desperately trying to accumulate enough money to make this purchase.

In addition to working ten-hour shifts at the mine these two young men took a contract to supply the big cookhouse with venison. From May through November they hunted deer by day and dug copper by night. All winter they ran a trap line. They also shot cougar and wolves at every chance. These skins were sold in Vancouver at good prices the following spring.

In 1906, the rich Mount Sicker copper deposits came to an end. Test holes were drilled for miles in every direction with little or no success. The young Holman family moved onto their newly-purchased land by the Chemainus River.

The big smelter at Crofton was closed forever in 1908. When the mines ceased operation it was only a matter of weeks until Mount Sicker became a ghost town. The daily horse-drawn stage coach from Westholme to the mountain top ended. The narrow gauge railroad that clung to ledges where sheer cliffs dropped hundreds of feet to the canyon below was abandoned. The building of this short-lived rail line was considered to be the toughest engineering feat of that decade.

To manoeuvre the shays pulling ore cars over this route needed men with nerves of steel and courage to match. Albert, for a time, was one of these men.

In 1912 the railway tracks were torn up. The ore cars were smashed up and shipped with the rails to be sold as scrap in Vancouver. Most of the mine buildings and all but a few of the family houses were demolished by storms and collapsed under the heavy snows. The little church with its steep roof weathered best of all.

In 1922, the Lenora Hotel was sold by auction. Mr. Ed Pinson, a cousin to the Holmans by marriage, with a bid of two dollars, became the new owner. He also bought several other buildings at one dollar each. He then negotiated a contract with Holman and Boudot to salvage the lumber and haul it down the mountain.

Some of these quaint old miners' houses were cut into sections and hauled out by team and wagon. Several were reassembled and set up along Mount Sicker Road. Some are being lived in at the present time and look good enough to last another 50 years.

Albert and Pete took lumber, doors and windows as part payment for their work. They improved their barns and other buildings on both properties, then went into the dairy business. Mrs. Holman continued to milk up to a dozen cows by hand and deliver milk and cream to Duncan until she was well into her eighties. Albert trapped fur and hunted cougar during the winter months. The Chemainus River offered a never-ending supply of mink, otter, beaver, raccoon, bear and muskrat. The mountains supplied marten, wolves and cougar.

In 1920, because of his experience, Albert was selected by the government as the designated predator hunter for the Chemainus River district. In 1922, the cougar bounty was increased from $25 to $40. That year a record was set for the most cougar ever shot in British Columbia. The previous high of just more than 200 jumped to a whopping 372.

Experienced hunters knew that the average cougar killed at least a deer every week. Multiply 372 by 52 and the result is 19,344 deer saved. The extra money paid out in bounties proved to be a good deal for everyone.

Frank, the baby of the Holman family, was born in 1923. Now the family was eight, five boys and three girls. Evelyn and Mabel, the two eldest, were already married when this youngest brother arrived. Then came Henry, Dolph, Kate, Doug, Fred and Frank. Henry and Dolph were young teen-agers and going with their dad on bounty hunts.

As the only official predator hunter Albert handled hundreds of calls at all hours of the day or night. Young Doug was about old enough to be taught the tricks of the trade. By the time he was 11 years old he could shoot the eye out of a cougar at 50 yards.

Things were going well for the Holmans until the early 1930's. The government dropped the cougar bounty to 10 dollars.

"Can't even buy dog feed with that kind of bounty money. If we catch some alive we can sell'um to a zoo for a 100, bucks or more," Albert told Dolph and Henry.

"We'll be on the lookout for a den or small tracks," Henry said, catching on quickly.

"If you find something, just mark the spot. Don't try to catch one by yourself. Come home and we'll all go after it together."

Late that fall Mount Sicker got two feet of snow on the upper levels. Dolph and Henry were hunting deer when they came on two sets of cougar tracks. One was an adult and the other half grown. They followed a short distance and came onto a freshly-killed doe.

"Those two devils won't leave this. We better get home and tell Dad," Henry suggested.

"We maybe could catch the young one. Not much bigger'n a dog," Dolph said excitedly.

It was too late to do anything but get ready for an early start next morning. Henry and his dad drove down to the Indian Reserve where Bonsall Creek runs into the saltchuck.

They borrowed some heavy salmon seine netting from Billie Thomas.

"Bring it back tomorrow, and thanks," Albert said as he started backing out the narrow drive. At home they picked up a couple of strong sacks and some rope from the barn. Henry and Dolph laid out heavy gloves and pants.

Laurence Stewart had been courting their sister Kate for more than a year and he arrived in time to get in on all the excitement. He hadn't been on a cougar hunt like this one. The four men with two hounds and all their cougar-catching gear were on their way early next morning. Big Henry was in the lead following the broken branches that marked the trail.

Dolph and his dad each led a hound. Laurence, with an ax and pack, had his work cut out just to keep up with the three Holmans. When they came to snow near the timber it was easy to backtrack to the deer.

Albert waved Henry to wait for Laurence to catch up. "Where's the deer from here?" he asked in a whisper.

Henry pointed to a big fir not more than 100 yards ahead and said, "In some logs back of the big tree."

They were looking at it and listening when the hound Dolph was holding put his nose up and began sniffing. He gave out with something between a whimper and a whine. Albert whispered just loud enough for the boys to hear, "Cougar feeding on that deer right now! Best we let the dogs loose and see what happens."

Both hounds charged toward the big tree. There was a short noisy chase, then a steady bellowing.

"They got one up a tree," Henry shouted as he ran through the snow-covered thicket. The old female was 30 feet up a hemlock glaring down at the barking hounds.

"Might as well let Laurence do the shooting. He's never killed one before," Albert suggested.

Henry handed him the 32-Special and said, "Shoot the bastard right in the heart, behind the front shoulder."

Laurence was so excited that he missed and hit the animal, breaking a front leg and knocking it out of the tree. Henry grabbed the rifle and charged in to protect the hounds. A short chase and a bullet through the neck. Henry was back in a matter of minutes dragging the dead cougar with a piece of rope.

"The young one is over there! Saw the track and heard him in the salal!" Dolph pointed excitedly.

"Put the dogs in there," Albert shouted.

The young tom flew up a tree with the hounds bellowing close on his heels. The tree was about a foot in diameter with no branches for a long way up. He was clinging to the trunk some 40 feet up, twitching the end of his tail and growling.

As they stood figuring what to do next, Albert said, "He won't jump from there. Henry, you get the ax and cut the tree down. Laurence, you and Dolph put on the heavy gloves, get that piece of seine net, then stand over in that opening. The bugger will probably ride the tree down. Trick is to jump on 'im and get 'im in the net without getting clawed or bit. I'll hold both dogs ready in case he gets away."

Albert put both hounds on leash and stood where he could direct the unusual proceedings. Henry had finished the undercut and was starting to chop on the other side. The cougar decided to scramble another 15 feet higher. Albert waved for Laurence and Dolph to move farther away from the tree. They had to be in the right place if they were going to nail that young critter. About 20 feet apart, they waited.

As the tree started to fall the cougar moved around the trunk. Now it was riding on the top side. That young cat rode the tree almost to the ground. Laurence and Dolph were ready to jump in with the net and hold him down until Henry and Albert could get some ropes on him.

When the tree was almost to the ground the little devil leaped right over Dolph's head then ran like hell for the bushes. Dolph grabbed for a foot but couldn't get a good enough grip to hold him. Albert let the hounds go. In nothing flat, they had him up a small bushy cedar with limbs almost to the ground.

A short conference. They decided Laurence should climb up and try to get a rope around its neck or a front leg. The young cougar, snarling and growling, batted the rope away. It climbed higher with Laurence following. When they were near the top the spindly tree bent over under the added weight.

"Pull his tail! Pull his tail!" Henry shouted.

Laurence wrapped his legs tight around the trunk, grabbed the cat's tail in both hands and gave a hard yank. The young cougar piddled on Laurence's head and leapt out into the snow. Henry dived at it. Dolph grabbed it around the neck and managed to keep the head turned out so it couldn't bite. Henry got a bear hug on it from behind, holding its front legs against its chest. He squeezed so hard it couldn't breathe. When the cougar went limp Albert threw the net over it and closed the opening with some wire. They put this snarling kicking bundle of dynamite into a heavy sack and tied the top with a rope. While they were skinning its mother the young one kicked around enough to tire itself out.

Big Henry put the sack of cougar on his back and headed for home. Everything went fine until he stumbled and fell against a log. The young cougar's claws slashed through the sack and through Henry's mackinaw to draw blood, inflicting four-inch gashes down his back. That ended the back-packing.

Laurence cut a stout pole 10 feet long. Using ropes, they slung the cougar, sack and all, to the centre of the pole. Henry took the lead end and Dolph the other for the rest of the trip home.

Curious neighbours and relations were at the house. Henry cut the ropes from the pole. Teeth and claws poked out. When the sack began to growl and bounce around the yard everyone moved back. Dolph and Henry cautiously manoeuvred this dangerous package of sacked cougar so one end was inside the barred door of the sturdy cage. Albert slit open the sack and one leap put the young tom in the back corner.

In spite of the heavy gloves and clothing Dolph suffered with a bitten knee and he and Henry were badly scratched. Laurence didn't smell too great for several days.

The young cougar was too old to tame. It would stay in the dark end of its cage all day and come out to eat and drink only after dark. In the early morning it would call five or six times. The call could be heard a mile away. It was like a shrill bird whistle and always sounded as if it was right beside you. A cougar is a natural ventriloquist.

Some months later arrangements were made to move the young animal to the Calgary zoo. I've been told the Holman's received expense money plus $150 for their trouble. They kept in touch with the zoo for several years. The family had grown fond of the young cougar during the few months they cared for it and they were genuinely concerned for its well-being.

It wasn't long after this unusual hunting trip that Kate became Mrs. Laurence Stewart. They operated a small sawmill and lived a short way down the road from the Holman family home. After their son Russell was born they got more land and started a farmers' market. They closed down the sawmill.

Laurence took a course in agriculture. With Kate's basic knowledge of growing things and Laurence's determination they have developed one of the finest gardens in the province. The market building with its ample blacktop parking lot is not only a tourist attraction but a credit to Vancouver Island.

It is indeed a refreshing pleasure to turn off the highway onto Mount Sicker Road, pick up some farm-fresh produce and have a friendly chat with Kate about old times.

Though it's now 50 years since Laurence helped bring in that live one, I'm quite sure that Kate is still partial to cougar hunters.

Born for the Woods: Doug Holman

As a young teen-ager Doug Holman had two main ambitions: to own a good rifle and to get a good logging truck.

In the summer of 1928 my brother Tom and I were boarding at the Compton farm at the top end of Mount Sicker Road. Charlie Parman had bought Compton's timber and moved in a sawmill. We were on his crew. He hired Doug's older brothers, Henry and Dolph. Tom, as head sawyer, had asked Henry to be his carriage man. Dolph worked with me as second faller.

Young Doug, 10 years old that year, was still at school. He spent that summer holidays camped out in the woods with his dad, Albert, and Captain Groves. They hunted cougar for the bounty at $40 per animal. Later, Doug told me, "It was better than the 25 cents a week I got for going early to light the wood stove in the school."

Wages in the late 1920's were low by today's standards. Tom, as head sawyer, was paid five dollars per day. This was tops in those days. He also got a bonus for all lumber

95

produced. As head faller, my take-home was $4.50 per shift. Dolph and Henry, the next highest paid, were on at 50¢ an hour. The rest of the crew worked for $3.20 a day.

Tom always shared his bonus money with Henry on a two-thirds/one-third basis. There would be six dollars to divide some days. These two husky young men were known throughout the industry as the best. The bonus money in itself set the stage for high production.

Mrs. Sweeney did the cooking and looked after the big farmhouse for Compton. She always had a batch of home brew perking in a crock behind the woodstove.

Board, including some beer, washing and mending plus our own private room, came to $30 a month.

In late July Tom and I had hurried from work to help bottle and sample a new batch. We'd barely got to the house when Compton rushed up to us, shouting, "Big black bear just left the hog pen, carrying a pig. Beggar growled at me and went off into the woods."

"We'll get Albert Holman to come up with his dog," Tom offered.

Mrs. Sweeney had the evening meal almost ready to put on the table, so she said, "I'll keep your suppers warm," handing each of us a bottle of beer as we headed for the Model-T pickup.

Young Doug and his dad had just finished supper and were sitting out on the porch when we drove into their yard.

"Big bear up at Compton's just carried off a pig!" Tom shouted.

Albert was out of his chair in a flash and giving orders, "Doug, get the gun! I'll get old Rags. Drive back in here, Tom, so you can turn," he said, pointing to an opening among the beehives.

We were on our way back to Compton's in minutes. Rags, an excitable Airedale, could smell the bear as soon as we

Albert Holman and Grace Richards. Wedding in Victoria, British Columbia, 1901.

Westholme School Class of 1925-26
Students from left to right

Back Row: Adam Nimmo, Gerald Griffin, Dick and Harold Nimmo. *Second Row:* Ed Devitt, Bruce and Joe Budot, Dolf Holman, Bud Sondergaard, Jim Nimmo. *Third Row:* Pearl Richards, Kate Holman, Joan Boudot, Kathleen Bonsall, Bobby Devitt, Eva Richards. *Front Row:* David West, Fred Bonsall, Frank (Bobby's dog), Charlie West, Dougie Griffin, Doug Holman.

The little dog belonged to Bobby Devitt. She had named him after the all-star centre forward of the Victoria Cougars when they won the Stanley Cup in 1924.

The teacher, Miss "Issa" Jones, now Mrs. R. T. M. Dobell of Maple Bay, remembers the year. Earlier, Dolf, standing third from right in the second row, had an infected sore below his right knee. After roll call one Monday, she asked his sister Kate why Dolf was not at school.

"Going to Chemainus to get his leg cut off this morning," she replied.

"Dolf needs both his legs if he's to have a decent life. I'm going up there and see if there isn't something more that can be done to stop the operation."

Leaving Eva Richards in charge of the class she rushed to the doctor's office in her old car... Mr. and Mrs. Holman, with Dolf, were already there. She managed to persuade Dr. Rogers to arrange for Dolf to see a specialist in Victoria.

After a delicate bit of grafting and patching-up, the healing progressed quickly. Dolf was up and able to leave St. Joseph's Hospital ten days later.

"That was 57 years ago," Issa mused when I visited her last fall, "Saw him only yesterday and he was walking on both legs. Better than most at seventy," she confessed.

All in a day's work, fall of 1914, at Westholme. *Left to right*; Miss Jennie Hughes, Evelyn, Mable, Henry and Dolf Holman. Behind Henry two big bucks. Dolf is in front of the cougar's head, Albert Holman rests his 30-30 against black bear. Kate is on Mrs. Holman's arm. Last on right is Grannie Hughes. Grannie was married several times during her interesting life. She was the mother of several of the people mentioned in this book. Grannie lived out the rest of her days on the old homestead.

Albert Holman and his youngest son Frank, 11, returning from a three-day hunt in the Jordan Meadows, 1934.

The five sons of Albert and Grace Holman, 1936. Left to right; Doug, Frank, Dolf, Fred and Henry, the oldest.

Kate Holman (now Mrs. Laurence Stewart) in her flower garden at Westholme.

Doug Holman with Steelhead, 1939. Largest fish weighed over 16 pounds. Caught in the Chemainus River. Physically Rainbow Trout are exactly the same as the Steelhead. The only basic difference is that the Rainbow live in fresh water. The Steelhead go out and live in the ocean. They return to the same river to spawn when they are three to four years old.

Doug Holman and his 1941 Diamond T logging truck in front of the Crofton Hotel. Log is from Mt. Sicker Road. The truck and trailer was purchased in 1944 for $5,500.00 from Blainie Clarke Logging Co. Doug, at 25, was already recognized as a reputable logger. Picture taken June 1946.

Doug Holman and his father Albert on the porch of their old farmhouse. A phone call from a neighbour, three miles further up Mt. Sicker Road, was all it took to finish the two predators. The bear had killed a pig. The cougar was shot in a pasture, stalking some young calves. The rifle is a .32 special. Westholme, British Columbia, 1947.   PHOTO: HOLMAN FAMILY

Albert Holman (nearing seventy), 1951, feeding one of the young bear cubs. He had shot over 300 cougars and put away many a troublesome bear by the time this picture was taken. He still enjoyed nature's wild creatures though he was no longer able to hike the long trails.

Amusing and being amused, Doug Holman at Westholme, 1951. He rescued the cubs near the Chemainus River.

Youngest Holman, "Frank," 1953. He has taken over 170 of these predators, most of them being problem animals, either molesting stock or prowling too close to settlements for safety. As a registered hunter, he would collect $160.00 for this weekend's work.

Frank Holman and Sandy Walker recently shot this cougar in the Chemainus area at the request of the Royal Canadian Mounted Police. This brings the total to 151 cougars they have been asked to hunt down. Photo taken in 1975.

rattled into the yard. The dog leaped over the side, practically pulling Albert out. They headed for the pig pen. From the pen we could hear all sorts of strange noises. Inside we could see some of the pigs staggering about, mouths open and squealing. Others were lying on their sides grunting contentedly. Some tried to stand but just reeled around and fell back into the mud again. Doug got the giggles. His dad walked over and picked up some mash out of the pig trough and smelled it.

"Pigs are drunker'n hoot owls!" he exclaimed. "Some fool dumped a batch of beer dregs in their trough! Hope the bear didn't get enough to make him crazy."

Albert let Rags go where the muddy bear tracks led into the woods, yelling, "That bear's packing the pig. He won't be far."

We soon heard Rags barking treed. We ran in and found the mangled pig scattered over the old Mount Sicker railway grade. Some 20 feet away we spotted the bear up a cedar tree, hanging on just out of the dog's reach. It leapt out of the tree and charged. Albert dropped him with a bullet in the neck.

Doug, proud as punch, unloaded his dad's rifle and climbed in the truck. What with the weight of the 300-pound bear plus Albert and me sitting on the tailgate, the rear tires went almost flat. We had to dig out the hand pump to put in more air before we dared start.

Tom and I stayed around at the Holman place to help hang the bear on the skinning tackle. Albert cut open the stomach and found the fermented mash.

"First boozed-up bear I've ever skinned."

Two days later Dolph handed me a four-pound jam can of bear grease, explaining, "Use that on your caulk boots twice a week. Keeps the leather soft and your feet dry."

A couple of years later Joe Kerrone started logging the timber off Mount Sicker. Times were tough and getting tougher when he moved his outfit from Cowichan Lake to start on the mountain. Kerrone was known as 'Gyppo Joe' from the early 20's until he died some 50 years later. Mr. Ferguson (Fergie) had the contract to haul the logs from the landing at the bottom of the hill to Crofton.

Young Doug decided he'd had enough education. He persuaded his parents to let him quit school, work on the farm and get whatever outside jobs there were. Doug would rush to get through the chores and wait at the roadside just below their house. He would hitch a ride on the logging trucks.

Four seasoned gear-jammers worked on this haul. Stan Brinham, John Luscombe and the Mitchell brothers. Stan was Doug's idol. He taught Doug everything he could about these primitive logging trucks. Air and hydraulic brakes were still a long way in the future. The braking systems in 1932 were all manual. Some had to be cranked on by a handwinch. The lower gears were much more reliable than the braking systems in keeping things under control.

The big depression had settled in deeply by 1933. Log prices were at an all-time low. Number 2 fir logs, boomed up, scaled and towed to Vancouver brought $8.50 for 1,000 board feet. Number one fir sold at $12.50. All hemlock and number 3 logs were left in the woods to rot. The sawmills would not buy logs with a smaller than ten-inch top diameter.

Gyppo Kerrone's most crippling and unpredictable expense was the number of cows killed by logging trucks. Many of the farmers' cattle grazed along the roadsides. Fences, if there were any, got little or no repair.

Kerrone called a meeting with the drivers, telling them, "Every time we hit a cow, the farmer claims top price. Says it was his best animal. If you fellows keep killing those cows, we're going to go broke, sure as hell!"

"Brakes won't stop the load on a hill," Stan Brinham shot back.

98

"Kill another cow, you pay for it out of your wages."

Next day Stan had an extra heavy load. Young Doug was riding with him. When they broke over the top of a hill the big load started gaining speed, fast. Stan had all he could handle to double clutch and shift to lower gears. The truck was almost out of control as they swerved around a corner. Two cows right smack in the middle of the road.

They were in the normal bulling stance, head to tail and tail to head. Stan laid on the horn. It made a noise much like a bull bellowing. The larger cow, with her back end toward the load of logs, mounted the smaller one and both began prancing about down the centre of the narrow road. Those two sex-crazed critters didn't even look toward the oncoming truck.

"Pull that emergency brake!" Stan shouted.

When Doug pulled back on the brake lever there was a snap and the handle went slack in his hands. No possible chance of stopping the truck. The gap between the rear end of the top cow and the radiator of the truck was closing fast.

"Now what?" young Doug shouted above the rattle and clattering of the big gas motor.

"Looks like the horny critter on top is going to get a rear end full of radiator, and quick," Stan yelled. "No other way!"

When the truck struck the top cow, it pushed her forward up on top of the smaller one's back. They fell, one on either side of the road. The rear wheels of the truck and both trailer wheels rolled over the cows. This did more to stop the truck than all the brakes and gear jamming. Doug leaped out.

"Got 'em both!" he shouted to Stan. "Dead as doornails."

Allen Broadie, owner of the two mangled animals, walked out on the road and stated flatly, "My two best show cows."

"I'll bet. I'll just bet they were," Stan said sarcastically.

They dragged the mess off into the ditch, and Stan said,

"I'll have to try and get the truck to Crofton for repairs. Doug can stay and help you get these prize animals to your butchering shed. Looks like our crew will be living on hamburger for the next month."

The winter came on and the depression got worse. Gyppo Joe had to close the camp. Even with wages averaging less than 30 cents an hour he couldn't make a go of it.

Fergie moved back to Vancouver and became a successful truck distributor. The four drivers moved to Ladysmith, bought their own trucks and for the next 30 years did well hauling for Comox Logging. Doug started as a log hauler and soon became a successful independent logger.

Doug's younger brother, Fred, quit logging to go overseas in 1939. Frank, the youngest boy, now 16, finished school and went to work for Laurence Stewart, Kate's husband, in their sawmill.

Frank shot his first deer with a 30-30 carbine on Mount Sicker when he was nine years old. He was out with his dad late in the fall of 1932.

"There were deer tracks everywhere," he remembers. "We came into an open alder bottom. Fresh deer trails crisscrossed in all directions. We stopped where two of these came together near a big tree. Dad, with a stick, drew a map on some open ground. He made an X to show me where we were standing, then drew a circle to show me where he was going. I was so scared he might not come back I started to cry.

"Dad just patted me on the shoulder and said, 'Don't be afraid son. Just be quiet and keep your gun ready. I'm going to try to put a deer up one of these trails so you can shoot it. Don't worry, just watch. I'll be back in half an hour.'

"It was all very quiet and scarey after Dad vanished into the timber. A while later, a twig broke below. That was the only sound I heard until a big buck stood like a statue facing me on the trail. His head was high. I still remember the big horns.

"I aimed at the white spot under his chin and fired. The buck dropped dead. I heard Dad whistle and answered. When he walked up the deer trail a few minutes later a strange feeling came over me. In that half hour I had learned the true meaning of trust.

"Dad took me on many cougar hunts with old Rags. He let me shoot one the year I turned 11. It was up a tree not too far from our house. Dad handed me his 32-Special.

"'Shoot it in the heart just back of the front shoulder,' he ordered. 'A cougar's head is so round and smooth a bullet can glance off it. This might only stun the beggar enough to knock him out of the tree. When you and the dog rush in that cougar can come to and kill the both of you. Saw a couple of dogs die that way.' I took careful aim and one bullet did the job.

"The old Airedale treed another small one on that trip and we got him, too."

Doug remembers when he and his youngest brother were the only ones left at home. The rest of the children had married.

"After he'd passed 60, Dad's health began failing and his legs were giving him trouble. It was sad to watch such a woodsman and hunter not be able to do the things he did so well and loved to do.

"Mother milked her cows and kept pretty healthy but Dad got so he could hardly walk more than out to the barn and back. By the late 1940's, he was spending most of his days in the old rocking chair, sitting on the porch, just watching the cars pass by. Before long, he sort of just gave up.

"One evening I was sittin' talking to Dad when my brother-in-law stopped by to tell me he'd tracked a cougar down into Haggerty's Swamp near the Chemainus River.

101

"'You and Frank take your hound up there first thing in the morning, you'll probably get him.'

"There was four inches of fresh snow on the ground and we were on the cougar's tracks shortly after daylight. Frank had the gun. I put old Boosh on leash and followed.

"There were a lot of huge cedar snags in this swamp. The cougar tracks led us right to one of the larger ones. We could see where he had spent most of the night either lying in the snow or tramping round and round this hollow tree. Old Boosh was making strange noises and tugging on his leash, trying to get going. Frank kicked the tree and we had a snarling bear snapping its jaws at us, not five feet away.

"'Shoot it quick! That's a hibernating bear and she's waking up fast.'

"The bear crumpled halfway out of its den, not more'n a yard from our feet. I let Boosh go. He paid the dead bear no attention. Just took off on the cougar trail, bellowing as he went. The cougar outran the dog for about three miles, then climbed a tree at the edge of the Chemainus River. Frank dropped him and then we dragged him back to the dead bear.

"When we pulled that bear the rest of the way out of its den, we heard squeaky "waaah, waaah" noises in the hollow tree.

"'Cubs!' we both shouted. Frank was on his hands and knees peering into the hollow. He stood up holding a tiny cub.

"'Tie the dog, there's another one in there!' Frankie shouted.

"He felt around and found the other one, way back at the far side of the hollow tree.

"They were only a few days old. Eyes are not starting to open yet. We'd have to keep them warm or they'd die.

"It was freezing cold and beginning to snow. I took the

two babies and put them inside my shirt. They wiggled around and made more funny noises, then went fast alseep. We were home in less than an hour. There was a cardboard box on the porch. Laying the cubs in this, Frank carried them into our kitchen. Dad was in his rocking chair by the woodstove.

"Mother took the box, wiped and dried the protesting young cubs, then put the lot on Dad's lap. She warmed some milk in a cup and found an eye dropper. Dad spent the rest of that day feeding and petting these noisy little creatures. He took on the job of looking after the cubs until they were almost a year old. I'm sure the little bears gave him great pleasure and a real reason for living. He felt useful and needed again.

"A month passed before their eyes were fully open. By then the cubs could drink from a bottle and nipple. Black bear cubs are natural scrappers. When they tire of wrestling each other they sleep for about half an hour, then pick a fight with anything that moves.

"In spite of kindness and the best care possible they were always looking for trouble. At about 10 months old we had to let them go to a zoo. It wasn't long before our house cats moved back from the barn. The house furniture got a cleanup and some repairs.

"By 1952 Dad was pretty crippled. He just gave up and died in August of that year. Frank had married and moved to his own place a year earlier. With just Mother and myself around to keep the farm going, it was pretty quiet.

"I did a lot of fishing and got to know the river well. It was because of the Steelhead runs each spring that I met and got friendly with Bill Sloan. He was in the process of taking over the management of all the timber owned by the E & N Rail way grant.

"I'd applied for a small block of blow-down away up the

Chemainus River to the north of Mount Sicker's old copper mine. We'd arranged to meet at the Westholme store around 10 a.m. on a day in late April. As usual I was up at daylight. To put in the time I headed for the river. By nine o'clock, I had hooked half a dozen nice Steelhead, released four, put two of the best in a wet sack and laid them in the pickup. Then I went to get Bill. We drove up as close as we could to the timber, put on our caulk boots and proceeded to walk over the blowdown.

"Bill hardly said a word as we looked. We were leaning against the box of the half-ton pickup preparing to change shoes when I pulled the sack off the two Steelhead.

"'What do you think of those babies?'

"Bill gave a low whistle, felt the fish with his finger, then smiled for the first time that morning and asked, 'Where'd you get 'em?'

"'Down the river. There's lots in right now.'

"'I've got my rod in the car. Can we have a try today?' he asked excitedly, and I said sure.

"My rod and reel hung in the cab, back of our heads. Bill got his out of the trunk of his car and we were on our way.

"There was about a mile to walk to the river from where we'd parked. I lead the way. It was rough going. Bill had somehow put his rod together and was ready to fish on the way down. He was that eager.

"'Put on a bit more lead and shorten your leader about six inches. Here's some sure-fire homemade bait. Use this gob of fresh roe.'

"We scrambled over the slippery rocks to a deep pool with four-foot falls pouring into it. He looked at me for more instruction. There was a huge boulder showing at the lower end of the pool.

"'Cast across, upstream and let your bait drift down in

104

front of the rock. Then drift past it on our side. Fish usually lay right in front of the rock.'

"His first cast was good. As the bait drifted in front of the rock, there was a flash of silver and he was into a 10-pound, fresh-run doe. With a bit of coaching he played the Steelhead well and slid it up near the gravelly shore.

"'It's not ready to come in yet,' I warned him.

"Bill gave me a look, kept his rod tip high and over the beach and waded into the ice-cold water almost up to his waist. He sort of herded the big fish up onto the beach. Finally, he put his caulk boot against its side and sort of kick-lifted it some 10 feet away from the river. Then he put one foot on either side of his prize, held the rod high in his left, then stuck his right hand out in my direction for a handshake. That was the start of a long and pleasant friendship. We hooked and released four more Steelhead that afternoon.

"We made a date to fish the river the following week. Bill asked if he could bring his friend Jack Roach along.

"The three of us walked the same trail. Bill was last. When we slid down the bank to the river he was completely rigged and ready to fish. Jack and I both looked at him with considerable surprise.

"'Try the same place again.'

"Before Jack got ready Bill had hooked and landed one fish, released another and had a third one on his line. Jack had been paying more attention to Bill than he was to his own gear.

"'This has got to stop,' he told me quietly. Picking up a pair of small snippers from his tackle box he walked up behind Bill, reached around and cut his line off just in front of the reel. The Steelhead took off down the river with the line and gear. It gave one mighty leap as it went over the shallows.

"'You no-good bastard! I'm going to throw you in the river,' Bill shouted, as he chased Jack back to where he could stand behind me for some protection.

"'Gentlemen usually wait until everyone is ready before they start fishing,' Jack chided.

"Jack and I laughed so hard our sides hurt and finally Bill joined in.

"When we were all ready to fish Jack produced a thermos of hot rum and suggested it was time for a mug-up.

"After a hot drink and a sandwich, Bill announced, 'I'm going to fish down river from that big log. That way I'll be able to push Jack in if he comes near me again.'

"'Thought you two were friends.'

"'We are,' Jack laughed. 'No one but a friend would dare cut Bill's line off.'

"A few minutes later, we heard Bill yelling for help. He had hooked into a big fish up river from the log and it had come downstream, gone under the log and had his light rod bent double.

"'What do I do now?' he shouted.

"'If you want that fish, you'll have to go in after it,' Jack yelled back.

"With a determined expression on his face, Bill leaped off the log into about five feet of white water. When he came up, he was 15 feet or more down river from the log, reeling in the slack line like a mad man.

"He bounced about in the rapids, going down river faster than Jack and I could run. When we caught up to him a quarter mile further down he was standing on a sandbar near the side of a big pool. He still had the fish on and was bringing it to shore.

"When the big doe lay over on her side we could see a dark band of red along the belly. Bill took out a pair of pliers and snapped the hook out of the fish's mouth.

"'Go finish your spawning. That was a great fight you put up,' Bill said as he gave it a boost with his foot.

"'That's the kind of conservation we need,' I told him.

"'I'm proud of you,' Jack said with a grin.

"When I drove them to their car and was putting the four fish in the back Bill tapped me on the shoulder. When I looked up he said, 'Better start logging that timber before the bugs get into it.'

"We all laughed and they drove away.

"That's about 30 years ago. There have been many other fishing trips and a few timber deals. I showed Bill how to blow salmon eggs out into the water with my mouth so it didn't scare the cutthroat trout in Bonsall's Creek.

"We had many good trips to the Cowichan and Koksilah Rivers. The big Springs in the salt chuck also got plenty of attention during the summers.

"Bucktailing for Coho in the fall at Cowichan Bay we considered a sport for kings. My older brother Dolph was a fishing guide and often went with Bill up to Rivers Inlet for the 60- and 70-pound Spring salmon that go up the river to spawn there in July and August.

"I also showed and explained the fish trails in the rivers to Bill. My dad had explained the trails to me when I was 10 years old. I've watched them for 50 years and learned.

"In the Chemainus River there are some places where the river bottom is all white sand. During the summer months when the water gets low and slows down it drops a lot of dark sediment all over the bottom. The Spring and Coho start going up to spawn long before it rains enough to wash this silt away. The water is clear as crystal when it is low like this so every mark is easy to see from the bank or a canoe.

"Most people think the fish just swim up a river all over the place. They don't. They have trails like deer, sheep or cattle do.

"The trail is about four feet wide and easy to see because all the dark sediment is swished off the sand by the fishes' tails as they move on upstream. I've watched hundreds of times and it is rare to see a salmon or trout travelling anywhere but along the trail unless they are spooked. I can tell just by looking at the trail almost how many fish are upriver.

"Bill poo-pooed this idea at first. When I called him to come up fishing because the trail was fresh and well-used he had to agree when we got fish."

When it comes to cougar and deer hunting, Doug got his experience at an early age. He started going with his dad and Captain Groves at age 10. Groves had two red hounds he had imported from England, Winnie and Zinger. They would not leave if they had a cougar up in a tree. Doug remembers a time they had been called to Crofton in the night. A cougar had killed several of Captain Bailey's sheep and ripped their dog up pretty badly:

"We put our hound Boosh in the back with the two red ones when Captain Groves came to get Dad and me to go along. When we got to Baileys', Dad looked at their wounded dog and told them to put it out of its misery. Most of the skin was torn off its head.

"'That's going to be a mean one,' Groves warned us.

"Next, we went with our three dogs on leash to where the sheep had been killed. The dogs got so anxious and excited that Dad decided to let them go. The cougar crossed the Crofton Road and we heard them barking treed, a mile up in the woods to the west.

"They suggested I go and see if it really was a cougar. He and Dad were not so young and didn't like travelling in the woods after dark. I ran up to the baying dogs without a gun. The cougar was crouched on a big limb about 60 feet up. I tied my coat to the tree and ran back to the truck. Dad waited there while Groves and I made our way back, using a weak two-cell flashlight. Groves fired twice but said he couldn't see the sights properly. He handed me the 30-30. I took the cat just behind the ear and he rolled off the limb, stone dead. We dragged the cougar out. He weighed better than 100 pounds. It was well after midnight when Captain Groves dropped Dad and me at home."

"How did you find things after your dad passed away?" I asked.

"A bit lost and lonely for a while. He had taught me well. We shot more than 100 cougars together. I was busy logging and helping Mother with the farm. Time passed quickly to help heal the loss.

"I guess, because it was so quiet around home, Mother became an ardent car racing fan. For almost 15 years, we went every weekend to watch these noisy competitions. It was about the only sport Mother got excited about."

Another Way to Log

In September of 1936 brother Tom and I were having a cold beer in the Elks Club at Duncan after a day on the job. Ted Robson and George Syrotuck who were part of our usual hunting party came in to join us. Ted had just come back from West Redonda Island where he and the Olmsteads were partners in a logging camp. It was Thursday and the deer season was to open Saturday. We always hunted together the first day so we were deciding where to go.

"That island is full of deer. I could have shot a dozen good bucks if the season had been open," Ted told us.

"Why not take your boat and run out there for a couple of days?" Tom suggested. "Where do you keep the camp boat?"

"Tied up at Campbell River. Takes only a couple of hours to get out to Redonda Bay. There's extra beds in the bunkhouse or some of us can sleep on the boat."

"We could leave tomorrow right after work and be there before dark," George added.

"I'm having a bit of trouble cutting road plank. The Olmstead boys don't seem to be able to keep the head saw from heating up," Ted said.

"Hell! Don't worry about that! Joe and I will straighten things out for you in half an hour. All we'll need is a good file, a chalk line and a piece of oak for saw guides. We'll show the boys how to keep the carriage in line. That's likely most of the trouble," Tom assured him.

"For Christ sake, bring us a round of beer," George shouted. "I'd like to get home to line up that new rifle before dark."

"We can meet here at five tomorrow and drive up in my station wagon," Tom offered.

Next evening the weather was good and we were in the Redonda camp an hour before dark. We went out and fixed the sawmill. Mrs. Olmstead fried fresh salmon for a bedtime snack.

"What time do you hunters want breakfast?" she asked.

"About five would be great, and thanks for the mug-up," Ted said as he took a bottle of Crown Royal from his bag and we had a drink before turning in.

After breakfast of steak and eggs we rode up the two miles of plank road in the camp pickup. New fireweed was two feet high where the logging slash had been burned. There were so many deer practically every plant was stripped of all its leaves and flowers. We saw a dozen or more deer in the headlights before we got to the logged-off area. Ted parked in a landing to wait for daylight and advised, "If we each take a side road up toward the standing timber the deer will be moving up that way early. You should be able to take your choice of any size buck you want. Get in a good place and just wait."

By noon each of us had two nice bucks. Ted had taken another two-point for the camp cookhouse. In spite of their

111

numbers, the deer were fat. We dressed the lot and wrapped them in cheesecloth to keep the blow flies away.

"Ever see cougar out here?" I asked Allen Olmstead.

"Yeah, once in a while we see tracks," he answered, then pointed to the Airedale sleeping on the mat by the door. "That old boy makes us better than $160 a year in bounty money."

"Any wolves or bear on the island?" Tom queried.

"We've been here over three years now and I have yet to see any tracks other than deer, cougar, raccoons and the odd mink. We put out a few traps in the winter and do pretty well," Allen answered.

We left camp early the same day and were back at Duncan in time to do a bit of bragging at the Elks before it closed. Bill Auchinachie was at the club and offered to skin and put the deer in his freezer for the weekend.

Off and on during the following 15 years we hunted on Redonda Island, always getting our limit.

On Thursday, March 5, 1959 I flew to Powell River to meet Jim Anderson and his partner Gordon Bell. They were handloggers and were wanting to sell their timber holdings near Gloucester point on the northeast corner of West Redonda Island. We discussed price and other factors. Anderson was willing to fly up with me to look over their camp and show me the timber license.

Bell flatly said, "I'm not going back there again for any reason."

He didn't explain why. It was more of a declaration to Jim than to me. He did an about face, walked to his station-wagon and drove off.

"Aren't you two getting along?" I asked.

"Bell doesn't like our camp and has decided to call it quits. I'll show you why when we get out there," Jim answered, as he unfastened the tie-up ropes from our floats.

112

I climbed in and told Jim to shove her out and get aboard.

The aircraft was a Piper Pacer with a 150 hp Lycoming engine. On floats, C.F. JXH took off at 55 m.p.h. and had a working ceiling of 12,000 feet or more in cold weather.

It was only a 20-minute flight from Powell Lake to their camp. We landed in the bay and taxied in to tie up alongside a couple of boomsticks lashed together to form a float. A single boomstick was the only walk to get on shore. We put on our caulk boots. Those boomsticks were slippery. The tide was on the rise so the plane would be reasonably safe for the next few hours. The only danger would be a wind blowing out of Toba Inlet.

"Doesn't look bad," Jim said.

He unlocked the cabin. There was a wood cookstove, cupboards, a table with four handmade chairs and four camp cots made up with flannelette sheets covered by gray blankets. It was damp and it smelled of mice. Jim lit the stove, bailed some water out of a tin pail and put the tea kettle on to boil.

"It's getting on for 11 o'clock. We might as well look at the cruise maps, have some tea and dry the place out a bit."

The shack had a veranda full length facing the bay. The roof was hand-split shakes. There were two small windows, one on either side and a shiplap door leading in from the porch. The outside walls were shiplap covered with black roofing paper fastened every two feet by split cedar strips about four inches wide. The floor was one ply shiplap and looked like it was about worn through in front of the stove and table. The shack was 12 by 20 feet.

"Not much room for a crew," I said.

He nodded agreement, as he opened a can of pork and beans, dumped them into a cast iron frying pan and put it on the stove to heat. He took rye crisp from the cupboard.

"Mice got into the butter so this is lunch," he said with a grin.

113

From the porch, Jim pointed to the northeast corner of the claim and explained, "The southeast corner is half a mile south of there on a bluff above Waddington Channel. To the west, the claim is about a half mile deep. Then there is more government timber that can be put up for sale. We might as well walk through to Doctor Bay and back. Not more than a couple of miles each way."

"I'll take the maps along so I can show you where we are." He lifted his 30-30 from its pegs over the door and handed me a cruising axe.

"Planning to shoot a deer?" I asked.

"There's few if any deer left on this part of the island. Damned cougar have just about cleaned them out."

Jim led off up a steep trail at a fast walk for a man his age. He would be about 70. It took us two hours to get across to Doctor Bay and back. The timber was good quality but very patchy and scattered over the rocky terrain.

"What's with your partner?" I asked Jim as we stood on the porch. "He seemed determined not to come back here."

"Well now that you've had a look at the timber I'll tell you what's wrong. Couple of weeks ago I took our boat down to Lund to pick up supplies. Gord was cooking his supper. The door was closed. He went to glance out the window and came face-to-face with a cougar looking in from the porch side. When he went to bed that night his two house cats were sleeping on one of the bunks. They could go in and out by the flap in the bottom of the door. That bloody cougar had waited and killed both cats as they went outside. The killer must have carried them away to eat. There was nothing left on the porch but some blood spots.

"When I got back next day, my partner had decided to quit. That's why she's for sale," Jim admitted.

We chatted a bit about winds and booming problems and

I asked, "Would you be willing to work for us and look after the logs once they are in the water?"

"I'll do the booming for a year, maybe more, if my health stays good," Jim promised. "I'll also go with you to the timber sale we have put up. That will be in Vancouver on March 17. If we are there there won't be any competition from the local loggers bidding the price up. Bell and I have logged around here for 40 years and have a lot of respect in the industry."

"I don't like the cougar either. One of the bastards dragged my Labrador from under this cabin less than a month ago and ate it."

When I left Jim at Powell Lake I handed him a cheque for $1,000 and I said, "This cheque is dated for March 21. If we get the timber sale at upset price you will have the balance in full as soon as the paper work can be completed." We shook hands and agreed to meet in Vancouver on Monday, the 16th of March.

Jim and Gord had done their lobbying well. There was no competition on the timber sale. Jim bid the upset. I raised the hemlock five cents and that was it. The papers were drawn up. Anderson and Bell had their full payment by the end of the month and seemed satisfied.

Jim did the booming for the next two years. He quit because his feet and legs were giving him some trouble. Small wonder at 72!

We moved in a new cookhouse and a couple of bunkhouses to Doctor Bay. As strong winds blew down Toba Inlet we could see trouble where Jim had built his camp. Those winds could come at you from the icefields at over 100 miles per hour.

The terrain was much too steep for the conventional cat and arch. We designed and fabricated an integral arch for a new D-8 Cat and sent it out on the scow with the camp buildings. This was "a first" for this particular type of logging equipment.

The Finning Tractor people advised us all guarantees were null and void if we continued to operate on such steep ground with all that weight on the back end of their machine. The letter was signed by Earl Finning, the president. After reading it for a second time I picked up the phone and called him person-to-person. Following a brief exchange about the weather and business in general I asked him exactly what parts of his D-8 he was worried about.

"The two rear track rollers and the driving sprockets," he said without hesitation.

"Send us a letter stating that and we will keep the machine. It's working just great on grades up to 40 percent and better," I informed him.

"The letter will be in the mail today," and I thought I could hear his laugh as he hung up.

Yarrows Shipyard in Victoria engineered and prefabricated the main parts of the arch. We had to bolt it onto the back end of the cat and design steel supports anchored to the front end of the cat frame. This piece of equipment was completely successful and paid for itself in less than a year. That D-8, complete with arch, cost us less than $60,000 in April of 1959.

(Finning Tractor in Nanaimo quoted a price of $415,535 for a 1984-D8L which is a later model model but similar in size.)

It was terrible terrain for cat logging. Joe Getz was operating. Don Pitt tended hook and bossed the show. Bill Auchinachie did the falling with the help of a big Swede we'd hired from Powell River.

We had to weld a heavy steel guard around the back of the cat and arch to stop the logs from shoving Joe out of his seat on some of the steeper grades. There were ledges and dropoffs all over that part of the island.

In May Auchinachie felled a tree along one of these ledges. There were some overhanging rock and caves on the top side. He was walking down to cut off the top when a cougar jumped onto the same log.

"It came at me hissing with its ears flat and mouth open. Those big teeth looked pretty dangerous at a distance of 10 feet or less. Even with the power saw at full throttle, she kept coming at me," Bill told us. "I backed up for 50 feet or more before the bitch stopped and she just stood and snarled at me. After I had stepped off the log at the butt end she turned and stalked back to where I had first seen her. She leaped off on the top side and went out of sight under the overhanging rock cliffs. When I shut off the saw I could hear her growling and rustling about in the salal. My Swede bucker, when he saw that cougar, took off down the hill and didn't stop until he had locked himself in the bunkhouse.

"Next morning Don and I took the gun up to see if the old bitch was hanging around. We didn't see her but when we explored under the overhang rocks we found where she had her den. There was a partly-eaten raccoon and plenty of kitten signs. I figured she must have carried them away during the night."

I was there with the plane that day. The Swede put his suitcase and other belongings in the back seat, climbed into the front and sat there. When I was getting ready to go he opened the side door to say good-bye to Don and Bill. He looked pretty shaky.

"Yesus, Yoe, she's no good. I go fur Powell River and no come back," and Don laughed but Bill didn't. He'd had quite a scare that afternoon.

The cougar bounty had been suspended for three years. Many of the hunters that had kept hounds and collected

117

bounties could no longer afford to buy feed for their dogs.

Redonda became overrun with cougars. Even when there was snow it was unusual to see any deer tracks. It was not uncommon to find five sets of cougar tracks crossing the truck road.

It got so bad our cruiser and road engineer would not go into the woods without pistols. Grant Hawthorne was followed many times, and he said, "It's not a nice feeling when you have to go back on your own trail to check something and find fresh cougar tracks in the snow not more than a 100 feet behind you. I'm taking my 45-colt along. At least I'll have some chance if it comes to a showdown with one of those sneaky bastards."

On two occasions I was helping Grant when we spotted cougar watching us. One was crouched on a rock ledge not 30 yards ahead and above us. The next time, a big female was standing on a cedar windfall about 75 feet ahead watching the trail we were following. Both seemed to be more curious than afraid. Grant asked me to try to get the government hunter to come over and shoot some.

On Saturday, March 28, 1959 I called Jim Dewar in Nanaimo. I offered to fly him in with a couple of hounds from Campbell River if he would come out and shoot some cougars.

"You can stay in the camp for free and the flying both ways can be charged off to road layout," I added.

Jim checked his notebook and replied, "You know, Joe, I'd like to get out there and thin those bastards down a bit for you. The trouble is, since the department stopped paying bounties, cougar are increasing everywhere. Right now I should be in three different places. There's a call from Sooke, one for Duncan, and an urgent one at Kelsey Bay. A young cat there is hanging around the school. I'll have to drive most of the night to be there by morning. I was just about ready to leave when you phoned."

"I'll try you again in the fall and see how things are," I suggested.

"Take some guns out there and shoot everyone you see. You're allowed to do that if they are bothering your stock," Jim explained.

"The only stock we had out there was a tabby cat with six kittens. They didn't last a month. Cougar caught every one. Came right into camp to take them from under the bunkhouse."

Jim laughed, and answered, "Maybe we'll get some more help by fall. I'll give you a call if things get better."

On the next flight back to Redonda I took in two rifles and the .45 pistol for Grant Hawthorne.

Jim Anderson shot two young cougars in one week on the beach not a 100 yards from camp.

"They were either looking for food or just watching me work," Jim told me. "Both were in poor shape. Skinny as rakes. Nothing in their stomach but a few bits of some crabs. I saw a bigger one the next day. It was after a mink that lives at the head of the bay. Could have been the mother of the other two," and added he often saw cougar walking along the beach south of camp when he was headed home in his speedboat. He hadn't been able to get close enough for a good shot.

It was the last day of April, 1959 when Denis Hagar phoned and offered me some shares in a new company. He was in stocks and bonds and a director of Pacific Western Airlines. The company owned several small Bell helicopters, and was forming Pacific Helicopters Limited to take over the chopper business and do charter work all over British Columbia, but especially on the coast. It sounded like a good idea. We could use these whirly-birds to good advantage at timber cruising and road location. Being a bush pilot and hunter, I thought a helicopter with a good pilot and a marksman with him could thin out those cougar on Redonda.

When I called Jim Dewar to tell him about the plan he seemed a bit surprised and a little doubtful. After discussing the idea in more detail he suggested we try it.

"I'm too busy to get out there and don't know a thing about it."

"We'll let you know how it works out," I told him.

"If things turn out well, the game department might be interested in using some of your machines for game counts or predator control."

Denis called the next day to find out about my taking the share offer. Sure, I'd go along. When he heard about our cougar plan he told me they had a three-place chopper in Vancouver.

"I'll pay half and you pay half," he offered "That way, I'll get to be part of the action. All it will cost us is the fuel and the pilot's wages. Let's go this Saturday. The second of May."

We agreed to drive up to Campbell River and take off at daybreak. He would take a rifle and a shotgun with plenty of buckshot. We met and soon were flying low at first light over the beach about a mile south of our camp at Doctor Bay when the pilot spotted three cougar walking near the water. He dived the chopper at them. They ran for the trees. I didn't know a cougar could climb so fast. They literally bounded up some 50 feet and clung to the tree trunks. The pilot zoomed up and then made a sharp left turn. He put us down on the beach not more than a 100 yards from the treed cats. Denis put an end to the lot of them with three quick shots from his 306.

We flushed out nine more cougar in about two hours

flying. We could hover just above the tree tops and the wind from the rotor and the engine noise would flush out any animal. It didn't matter how dense the cover was. The cougar would usually run out, stop for a look, then disappear like a ghost.

On the open bluffs to the north of Teakern Arm we treed and shot a big tom. Out of the 12 cougar we saw, six of them climbed trees but the others took cover and lived.

That morning we saw only one deer on West Redonda. We covered more than 100 miles over what had once been the best deer country on the coast.

As we drove down the highway to Victoria, I said, "Do you realize we looked at enough inaccessible timber this morning to buy half of Victoria, if those logs could be put in the water and sold?"

"You mean, maybe we should try logging with helicopters?" he asked.

"If we could find a chopper big enough to lift just one good-sized log, we'd have it made, Denis."

The following week, the original five directors began planning on a project that was at least 20 years ahead of its time. These men were Jim Storie, Bruce Samis, Denis Hagar, myself and Bob Kincaid, a logger from Oregon.

This group did some inquiring and decided to have a good look at the Vertol 107 Chinook twin-fan chopper. It was to be powered by the first ever turbo engines for helicopters.

We left Vancouver Sunday, June 21, 1959 and were at the Vertol factory in Philadelphia next morning. Steve Tremper, their international sales manager, met us. We made a tour of the plant.

The most exciting thing we saw was two handmade turbo engines on a bench being prepared for the first Chinook to come off their assembly line. Bob Kincaid picked up the 2,000 horsepower motor.

"Weighs about 150 pounds," he guessed.

"A gas engine to do the same job would weigh 10 times as much," Tremper explained. "That in itself gives the Chinook a ton more payload than our present machines."

We were impressed and back home we had a meeting and decided to go ahead and try to select enough timber to start such an operation. Bob and myself were to be responsible for timber. Denis and Bruce would explore ways to raise $3,000,000 to buy three 107's plus parts, support shop and camps.

I hired Maurice Ayer and Ian McQueen to help with the timber aquisition. They were both forestry engineers and knew the procedures necessary to deal with the government bureaucracies.

The results of the timber buy was excellent. In less than a month we had located and mapped our 100,000,000 board feet of good timber. This had been approved and set aside by the forest service. Ray Williston, then the minister, had given us a letter confirming the necessary timber volumes to make this astonishing new venture economically feasible.

To make it short, Ian McQueen and I spent some 60 hours in the air using JXH on floats. He did the mapping while I did the flying. Maurice Ayers did the ground sampling. He bored holes into the tree trunks and weighed the little cores so we arrived at a fairly accurate weighing system. We also used a Bell helicopter to get us into places where the fixed wing was too fast and the mountains too steep for climbing on foot.

By September, we had looked at thousands of trees and deer and dozens of cougar, wolves and bear. We had covered all of the east side of Vancouver Island, most of the islands along the Mainland coast and all of the Mainland inlets from Jarvis north to Kingcome Inlet.

Believe me, Jim Dewar got a full report on cougar that

September. He told me he was still much too busy checking hunters and shooting the problem and dangerous meat eaters to get out to Redonda Island until next spring at the earliest. I let him know we had eliminated over a dozen cougar while we were cruising.

"That's good. Keep thinning them out."

Brother Ollie took over the ground logging a couple of years later on Redonda. He brought a black Labrador in with him. Prince was allowed to sleep in the cookhouse after a nasty fight with a cougar. He was doing a lot of growling and fussing around by the outside door one evening. Ollie figured Prince just wanted out so he opened the door. In the brightness, not five feet away, a big cougar was on the porch cleaning up the food that Prince had left in his dish. Ollie went for his gun but it was too late. Prince came out the clawed-up loser.

A week later, a smaller cougar followed Don Pitt along the boardwalk from the cookhouse to the bunkhouse. Don threw a stick and hit it in the ribs and the young cat growled and stalked away.

One of Ollie's logger friends was swinging logs from a colddeck pile to the beach on East Redonda. This was about a mile across Waddington Channel from Doctor Bay. As it was only a two-man show they were camped out in a tent on the beach. One afternoon the two men roared into the bay in their little speedboat looking for Ollie.

"Get your gun and come with us. There's a mad cougar at camp," they shouted.

He told me about the incident the next time I came into camp. We taxied across the channel in the plane and tied up to a boomstick. About 200 yards up the swing road Ollie showed me the remains of the mackinaw coat and explained what had happened.

Bert had eaten his lunch sitting on a stump. He covered his

lunch pail with his mackinaw and left both there. He then drove the D-8 up for a turn. When he came down around the corner he saw this big mountain lion clawing and ripping the coat.

"Had its tail straight in the air," Bert said. "The damn thing started to climb up on the moving machine so I hit it with a pipe wrench."

I looked at the ripped coat. It was scattered about. We found no piece bigger than three inches square. Even the buttons were torn off.

Another example of how unpredictable a cougar can be. These last cases have never been reported to the game department for their records. Wonder how many more cases they don't know about?

An incident mentioned in the last chapter of Lyn Hancock's book, *Love Affair with a Cougar* describes vividly how her "Tom" (the cougar they had raised from a kitten to adulthood) had scratched a seven-year-old Indian boy at Fort St. James in central B.C. David, her husband, was on a tour showing films. He had taken their cougar along as an added attraction. Apparently, the young Indian lad had the smell of moose blood on his clothing which must have prompted the attack. The animal was shot.

On my travels up and down the coast of British Columbia I have always been interested in our native Indians and their carvings. There has never been a cougar carved on any coast totem pole, to the best of my knowledge.

Abel Joe of the Cowichan tribe says it is to do with spiritual things. I asked him to spell their word for the animal. He wrote it out "HUTLUO TSUN."

Government and Game

In just over 100 years there have been some great men involved in the many changes and widespread growth of our Fish and Wildlife Branch in British Columbia. Events of the past are:

- 1870. A game ordinance was passed that dealt only with trespass and bounties.

- 1873. A game amendment was passed to deal with bounties.

- 1892. A game protection act came into being. Dates were set for open and closed seasons. The export of game was restricted and it became unlawful to shoot cow moose or hen pheasants.

- 1898. It became illegal to take trout under six inches except by children under 15 years. Dr. Helmcken introduced an act protecting certain animals and birds. It also became illegal to hunt deer with dogs.

- 1905. All the previous regulations were gathered together and put into the hands of Bryan Williams. He handled this responsible position and pioneered many aspects of game conservation until 1918. In 1905 it also became illegal to expose game for sale without the heads or birds without plumage.

- 1907. The wildlife branch received its first operational funds—$10,000 in total.

- 1910. The game branch was moved from "Lands and Works" and placed under the Attorney General's Department. A launch was purchased to patrol the coast. Moose, formerly unknown to the Interior, were increasing steadily and moving south and west.

- 1911. Deer were liberated on Queen Charlotte Islands.

- 1913. The first citizen's firearms licence was issued at $2.50, and 40,000 were sold. There were also over 7,000 free licences issued to land owners and farmers. Regulations were introduced prohibiting more than one shell in the magazine of pump or repeating shotguns. All automatic shotguns were prohibited.

- 1918. The Game Branch as such was abolished. Williams was retired on pension and the wildlife administration was placed under the jurisdiction of the B.C. Provincial Police. A Game Conservation Board was set up under the Chairmanship of Dr. A. R. Baker with five others on the board. Bag limits were reduced by as much as 40 per cent.

- 1924. Mountain goats were released on Vancouver Island for the first time.

- 1929. Great dissatisfaction was apparent between the police and the game associations. Williams was recalled from retirement and appointed B.C. Game Commissioner. James G. Cunningham and Frank R. Butler were appointed directors. Headquarters were moved from Victoria to Vancouver.

Probably the most important of all the changes was the regulation covering the registration of trap lines. Until 1926 this had been loosely regulated and created many arguments and court cases plus a couple of shootings. Most of the credit must go to Butler for these changes.

- 1932. A. G. Bolton was appointed fisheries supervisor. He started three trout hatcheries that year: at Qualicum Beach and Veitch Creek, the third was on the mainland. It became compulsory for the first time to tag all deer, and 14,838 tags were sold.

- 1946. Cache Creek checking station opened under the direction of Game Warden W. H. Cameron.

- 1947. The first annual Game Convention was held at Harrison Hot Springs. Dr. James Hatter became prominent at this time because of his studies of moose, relating to ticks and other parasites.

- 1948. Bonus cougar bounties were implemented and 725 cougar were turned in. This was 200 more than any other year on record.

- 1954. Twenty bighorn sheep were trapped west of Williams Lake on Sheep Creek Hill and transferred to Oregon. Commissioner Jim Cunningham died after a heart attack. His passing saddened everyone who knew him. He was indeed one of our greatest conservationists.

- 1954. Coyote bounties were suspended.

- 1955. Wolf bounties were suspended. It became legal to fish for trout in some lakes all year.

- 1958. Cougar bounties were suspended.

- 1962. Frank Butler retired.

- 1963. Dr. James Hatter was appointed director.

- 1966. Cougar and wolves were reclassified from predators or varmints to big game animals.

- 1973. Almost 6,000,000 trout were transplanted (mostly by float-equipped aircraft) into some 380 lakes. Game wardens enforcing all these new regulations had risen to 77 men.

- 1973. The first limited entry hunting was instigated. This was for residents only and applied to grizzly bears, mountain goat and sheep. A Senior Citizen licence for one dollar was introduced.

- 1974. Douglas Holman was prosecuted for shooting a dangerous cougar. David Hurn was promoted to assistant director for protection of fish. The total protection force increased to 110 and the fishing licence was raised from three to five dollars.

- 1975. The province was divided into 218 management units replacing the 28 units that had been used for many years. An atlas with maps of the units was printed. This atlas cost $5.95. It created great confusion.

- 1976. Dr. Hatter was named special adviser to the deputy minister. Don Robinson became acting director and took charge of the Fish and Game Department.

- 1977. Gross revenue from the sale of all hunting and angling licences plus other associated sources was $5,572,901. A new cougar regulation made it compulsory to submit the skull with lower jaw attached. A permit was now required to export cougar from Canada.

- 1980. A preliminary cougar management plan was started.
  When cougar became a big game species in 1966, there were many and varied ideas on just how this new regulation should be dealt with. The management plan created its own problem.

  Farmers and ranchers, especially sheep ranchers, wanted some answers as to how the game department

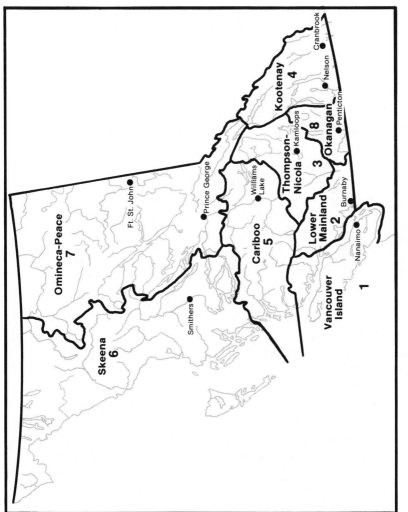

The Wildlife Management Regions of British Columbia

129

was going to handle the situations. They wanted to know just how to cope with a problem killer when it attacked their livestock off their own property. If this happened on leased land when the season was closed, would it be illegal to destroy such animals? Bears and wolves were in the same category as cougar.

It was decided to employ government hunters with trained hounds to deal with problem animals. However, there was too much area and too few government hunters to be satisfactory.

The game biologists produced a management plan in the mid 1970's. Although the plan was considered preliminary, it was most revealing to the average layman.

The plan declared cougar have no specific breeding season although April is the most common month for mating. The gestation period is 90 to 96 days. Females give birth to a litter of one to six kittens.

Cougar can live as long as 18 years but in the wilds 12 years is considered about the limit. Four litters in a lifetime was average.

The older males will kill and eat the young if they get the chance when the mother is away.

Jim Dewar, the experienced cougar hunter, said, "A female, no matter what species, rarely comes in heat while they are nursing or caring for their young. Probably some old tom found out about this several million years ago. If there were no young ones to care for, then the mother would accept his favours much sooner. This trait has been going on for so long it is now an instinct born into the males. They will kill and eat unguarded kittens up to a year old."

Deer are the cougar's principal food. The recognized average is about one deer per week for each cougar. However, beaver, raccoon, rabbits, dogs, house cats, grouse and chickens are considered to be part of their diet.

They have been known to kill and eat coyotes, lynx, bobcats, wolves and even their own if one is killed in a fight. Moose, elk, mountain goat, bighorn sheep, marten, mink, squirrels and birds of all types are food for a hungry mountain lion. Domestic animals of all types, as large as a horse and as small as a young kitten, have fallen prey to cougar. Sheep and dogs are the most common domestic prey. Even children have been mauled and in a few cases killed.

The game department admits the management of cougar is extremely controversial. Many people feel this animal should be totally protected. Others think it should be eliminated. The Wildlife Branch has decided to continue to investigate reports of predation and remove problem animals by relocation or killing them.

In 1983, a young tom was tranquilized near Alberni. It was collared with a beeper and released in the wilds to the west of Nanaimo Lakes. This young tom was killed by another cougar within a month. The beeper was still giving out signals when the carcass was found. It was lying near a creek 15 miles west of Cowichan Lake, 30 miles from where it was released. The only marks of violence were two big fang holes in the back of its skull. Certain evidence the killer was a cougar. Male cougars that have established their own ranges will not tolerate trespass by weaker animals unless the weaker animal is a female.

"In summary," the Wildlife Department admitted, "so secretive is the animal, it is the most rarely-seen big game species in our province. British Columbia has one of the densest cougar populations in North America. Vancouver Island and parts of the Fraser Valley are by far, the most concentrated."

131

The provincial cougar population in 1979 was estimated to be 3,300 animals—plus or minus 20 per cent.

Objectives of the management proposal:

- to maintain a viable cougar population in suitable habitat throughout its present range,
- to protect humans and reduce livestock losses through control of individual problem animals,
- to provide 3,000 hunter days of recreation with a sustained hunter kill of about 200 cougar.

Cougar will be managed as an integral part of wild ecosystems, generally being allowed to fluctuate naturally.

Harvest rates will be low, generally not exceeding 10 per cent of the population.

In some local pockets of dense cougar populations that occur near towns or where there is much livestock, the predator kill will go much higher than the 10 per cent anticipated. Problem animals in such areas will generally be destroyed rather than translocated.

A summary of management problems as concluded in 1979:

- Cougar near human settlements may attack people, pets or livestock! This animal may be attracted to human settlements and livestock areas because of declined wild prey numbers (deer, beaver, raccoon, etc.). Hunger makes them bold. Cougar populations cannot be maintained near human population centres.
- Inventory is difficult to conduct and is incomplete.
- There has been only limited biological research on cougar in B.C.
- Cougar can occasionally cause serious livestock losses.
- Expanding livestock production is increasing cougar-human conflicts in some areas.

In 1984, five years after this preliminary management plan was introduced, it is evident changes must be made again. Both cougar and wolf populations have grown out of control since these animals were classified as big game animals. The wolf population has virtually exploded on northern Vancouver Island. The deer herds have been reduced to less than 30 per cent of their normal numbers.

Dr. Hatter claims this is almost entirely the work of too many wolves. This drastic reduction of the blacktail deer herds, in his opinion, is a Vancouver Island deer crisis. Jim is a game biologist, a trained ecologist and a conservationist. He is recommending the use of 1080 as a means of control. Being a canine poison, it should be handled only by competent personnel using proper dosage. This would eliminate any great danger to non-target wildlife such as cougar, lynx, raccoon, etc.

I've been told that a man mistakenly cooked up a poisoned bait which he thought was his stew meat. He ate the stew and is alive today.

This bait, according to the experts, would have killed two fully-grown wolves in a matter of minutes. Don't get carried away; 1080 is certainly not being recommended for human consumption. There are a hundred better ways to spice up your camp stew.

Dr. Hatter believes any attempt to shoot or trap the wolves back to reasonable numbers is wishful thinking and a waste of time and money.

"The bush on the north end of Vancouver Island is much too thick and the area too large and rugged for that type of control."

When the deer are scarce, the cougar get bold and hungry.

The fall of 1981, some loggers were driving along a logging road near Telegraph Harbour and saw a big old wolf ambling ahead of them. It was carrying something.

They speeded up and the wolf dropped what he was carrying and jumped into the thick bush. Its kill was a cougar kitten. Not more than a month old.

I have hunted the north end of Vancouver Island for more than 10 years. It was no problem to have your pick of any size buck you wanted until 1980. Three years later you would be lucky to see a deer of any kind. Plenty of wolf tracks and droppings full of deer hair, though.

Deer hunters and people of all walks of life had better heed Dr. Hatter's advice. Organize and put pressure on the politicians. It is not too late to save some of the few deer that are left. The onslaught on deer by wolves must be stopped—NOW!!

Another grave problem is the known fact these wolves are carrying tapeworm parasites commonly known as a "hydatid" (Latin—*Echineoccus granulosus*). These parasites are being transmitted to deer. If you are lucky enough to bag some venison, you may also wind up with a dose of tapeworms.

To the best of my knowledge the Wildlife Branch has given no advice as to what precautions should be taken. Your dog could pick up the parasites by merely sniffing at wolf droppings.

There was also much publicity about the shooting of wolves in the northern parts of B.C. in the spring of 1984. The biologists and field men of the department believe it's absolutely necessary to reduce the wolf population in the north.

If it isn't done now, the moose, deer, elk and cariboo of northern B.C. could go the route of the blacktail deer on northern Vancouver Island.

The Collared Cougar Trial

On April 4, 1974 the *Cowichan Leader* published this letter-to-the-editor:

WRONG PERSON FINED

Editor:

Re: Cougar shot by Mr. Holman. Supposing someone, walking through the bush, found this cougar "snagged," hanging by the collar and dead from starvation. Supposing this was reported—I wonder if Mr. and Mrs. Dewar would have been fined?

It's cruel to put collars on cougars or any wild animal as this could happen.

I think the wrong man paid the fine.

Ada Cheleet

Sandy Walker remembers well the morning of October 21 in 1973. It was still frosty at mid-morning when he spotted Horace Mabley with two young boys hurrying toward the Walker house. Horace was visibly shaken and the boys very excited. They had rushed down the old Pipeline Trail, thick with salal and brush, from the Mabley home half a mile away—close neighbours for that area.

"Something killed our best ewe not 10 feet from our back porch last night. Could you come over and have a look at it?" Mabley asked.

"Whatever killed the sheep dragged it up the hill," the visiting English lad blurted out.

"Be with you in a minute," and Sandy stuck his axe into the chopping block by the shed, went to his house and came back with a rifle and shells.

Sandy's two cougar hounds were tied to their wire runs not more than 50 yards away. When they saw Sandy carrying a rifle the dogs surged at their chains and set up a loud bellowing. You could have heard them for a mile.

"I'll go ahead with the gun. You follow," Sandy directed. "The hounds will quieten down soon as we're out of sight."

"Maybe we should take 'em. It just might be a cougar," young Mabley suggested.

"We'd better have a look first," Sandy explained.

They moved up the trail at a fast walk. The boys rushed ahead at Mabley's gate and ran up through the sloping pasture and stood, one on each side of the dead sheep.

Sandy parted the wool on the neck and they could see the big teeth marks near the back of its head. The men rolled it over. Its chest had been ripped open. The heart and liver were gone.

"A cougar?" the English boy asked. "Did it do that?"

"Sure did," Sandy stated emphatically. "No other animal is strong enough to drag a sheep up this hill and leave such marks. Only a cougar covers its kill the way this is done, with some sticks and dry leaves."

"I'm going to get Doug Holman to have a look," Sandy stated. "He's shot dozens of cougar that have killed sheep. The most experienced hunter around."

"Keep the children and your dog in the house 'til I get back," he ordered. "That cougar could be dangerous."

136

"I'm not afraid," the boy from England said.

Sandy gave him a quick look and pointed up to where the sheep was covered and replied, "That sheep isn't afraid either. Anyone can see that."

Some 20 minutes later Doug and Sandy drove up the gravelled road in Sandy's four-wheel drive. Doug walked up the trail where the cougar had dragged the sheep. After one good look at the dead animal's neck, he told Horace, "Cougar's work. No doubt about it."

"What should be done?" asked Horace.

Doug said, "Let's phone the Fish and Wildlife office for Mr. Gosling. He's game warden and the only one who'll know what to do."

They agreed and went in to make the call. A clerk told Horace that Gosling was out of town and wouldn't be back until Friday.

"He's the only one with the authority to help," Doug said.

"Can you fellows dispose of the bastard?" asked Mabley.

"You say the word and we'll finish that killer in short order," Doug assured him.

"We certainly can't keep the children in the house all week. They have to go to school tomorrow," Mrs. Mabley stated flatly.

"It's not safe for kids to pass so close to that dead sheep with the cougar guarding it," Sandy said.

"I've never seen a cougar come 10 feet from the porch to kill. Must be something wrong with this one," warned Doug.

"Let's get my dogs and go after it," Sandy said.

Horace looked at his wife who nodded and he said, "Go get your dogs and kill the bastard! I'll be responsible! It's our sheep and our land."

At Sandy's place the two hounds were loaded into the back and Doug suggested, "Sandy, better we should see if my nephew is home. He's got a real good cougar dog. If this cat is as bold as it seems to be, three dogs will be a whole lot better 'n two."

Doug phoned his nephew—"Don't need a gun, just the hound and your pickup truck. Come on! A big cougar at the Mabley's place. Get there quick!"

Both vehicles got there about the same time.

"Keep your dog and the kids in the house," Doug shouted to Mrs. Mabley, then turned to the men and said, "Hold the dogs on leash until I tell you to let them go. I'll take the gun so's you'll have both hands free," and Sandy handed Doug his .300 Savage.

"Is she loaded?"

"To the hilt," Sandy said. "That's a four-power Bushnell scope. Shoots about an inch high at 50 yards."

Sandy walked ahead with his two hounds straining at their leashes. Doug followed closely, his nephew on his right with his dog.

The moment they got the cougar scent the dogs started whining.

Doug looked at his partners and said, "That bloody cat is right close. Turn 'em loose and see what happens."

The three hounds lit off up the hill, noses to the ground.

About 100 yards to the north a windfall had flattened the wire fence. As the dogs charged through this break the hunters saw a brown flash from under the log just outside the fence.

The hounds gave chase, streaking after the cat. Not more than 200 yards away the dogs were barking treed.

"Got'm!" Doug shouted as they rushed forward. He passed his nephew the gun and said, "Here, you carry this. You're younger'n me. I'm nearing 60 and don't travel as fast as I used to."

Sandy was first at the tree where the big cat crouched

about 40 feet up the bushy cedar. "Look, the son of a bitch has got something around its neck!"

"Let me look at it through the scope," Doug asked holding out his hand for the rifle. He studied the cougar and announced in surprise, "Something in its left ear, too. Looks like a cattle or hog tag."

"Let me have a look," Sandy ordered.

Doug passed over the rifle and remarked, "Maybe this one has escaped from a zoo?"

"It's a tag for sure!" Sandy exclaimed. "Plain as day. Maybe we shouldn't shoot it."

"Let me take a look," Doug's nephew demanded, reaching for the gun.

The big cat was now fidgeting about and moving its head from side to side.

"He's gonna jump! He's gonna jump!" Doug shouted. "Give it to him! Give it to him quick!"

The rifle roared and the cougar slid off the limb dead.

"Never knew what hit him," Sandy said. "The bullet hit him about an inch below the left ear."

They found both ears had a round tag. The left one was marked No. 7 and the right, No. 79. A radio-tracking beeper collar was bolted around the neck. Two short bolts held the ends which had been lapped over each other. The beeper collar had a number that looked like 7314. The batteries that had operated the tracking device were green and bulging. The animal's neck was raw and infected. It smelled like rotten meat.

Sandy, nudging the cougar with his toe, remarked, "We got ourselves an adult male. Must weigh more 'n 140 pounds."

Doug, checking the dead cat closely, felt the collar and ear tags and exclaimed, "My God! This damned collar must weigh more'n two pounds. Look at those ear tags. So heavy the cougar's ears are folded down on its head."

After they had dragged the cougar into the yard and stretched it out by the dead sheep, the two boys examined the big feet and claws, checked the teeth and felt the thick collar and ear tags.

The lad from England looked up at Sandy, his face troubled, and asked, "Isn't it kind of cruel for people to treat a wild animal like this?"

"Sure is," Sandy agreed.

The Mableys thanked their neighbours before the men threw the sheep killer into the truck.

The carcass was taken up to the old homestead on Mount Sicker Road. When the stomach was cut open it was found to be empty. Doug and Sandy came to the conclusion this tom must have been travelling with another cougar. The sheep's liver and heart had already been eaten before their cougar was shot.

News of the sheep killings travelled quickly around the neighbourhood. Many people, like the Mableys, had small five-acre ranches. A few sheep, a milk cow, some chickens and maybe a goat or some pigs would be all the stock they had. Usually surrounded by woods and well back of the roads, these people were naturally concerned for their children and animals.

An investigation by the game department followed. Gordon Gosling, conservation officer, apparently faced with public opinion versus proper government procedure, issued the following document:

MEMORANDUM Nov. 23/73

DEPARTMENT OF RECREATION AND CONSERVATION
FISH AND WILDLIFE BRANCH

MEMORANDUM

TO W. D. Haddleton

Regional Protection Officer

Nanaimo B.C.

FROM Gordon D. Gosling

Conservation Officer

Duncan B.C.

DATE Nov. 23, 1973   FILE No. 61-08

Information Re: killing of ear tagged and radio collared cougar.

1. About Oct. 28, 1973, Mr. Horace Mabley of 2542 Nimmo Road, Duncan B.C. (Westholme) had a sheep killed by a cougar. He contacted a neighbour, Sandy Walker, who has cougar dogs to remove the nuisance animal.

2. Mr. Walker and two freinds, Douglas and Harvey Holman, put the cougar dogs on the trail and soon treed the cat. While the cougar was up the tree they observed something around its neck.

3. Doug Holam shot the cougar. Inspection of the carcass revealed it was a male, tagged ine each ear (a number 7 and a number 79) and radio collared.

4. He took the cougar to his residence and skinned it. He stated that the pelt was of little value because it was "rubbed" where the collar had been.

5. He became worried that he might get into trouble for shooting a tagged cougar and burned the entire evidence; hide, ear tags and radio collar.

Doug Holman, who did the shooting, possessed a valid hunting licence but did not have a cougar tag licence. At this writing charges are being considered for either shooting a cougar without a tag licence or destroying government property.

Gordon D. Gosling
Conservation Officer

141

Common sense, it would seem, is one thing; government procedure sometimes another. Gosling was caught in the middle. On November 26, Gosling handed Doug Holman a summons ordering him to appear at the Duncan Court House Tuesday, March 5, 1974.

SUMMARY CONVICTIONS ACT

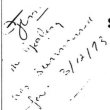

SUMMARY CONVICTIONS ACT
CRIMINAL CODE

FORM 2

Information

(S.C.A., ss. 10 and 17; C.C., ss. 439 and 695)

CANADA:

PROVINCE OF BRITISH COLUMBIA,

COUNTY OF Nanaimo

Regina vs HOLMAN, Douglas

This is the information of Gordon Gosling, a Conservation Officer acting on behalf of "Her Majesty The Queen".

of Duncan, British Columbia

hereinafter called the " informant."

The informant says that he has reasonable and probable grounds to believe and does believe that Douglas HOLMAN, on or about October 28th A.D. 1973, at or near Westholme in the Province of British Columbia, unlawfully did hunt wildlife, to wit: cougar, at a time not within the open season, contrary to form of statute in such case made and provided.

SWORN before me

this 26ᵗʰ day of

November , A.D. 1973 .

at Duncan, British Columbia

(Signature of Informant.)

In and for the Province of British Columbia.

143

Now there was one very dead sheep, one shot cougar, a batch of riled islanders and some very angry Holmans. Doug was known to be a man of his word. He had not been in court before. He decided to get a lawyer and retained J. G. Harvey of Duncan. The Crown prosecutor for the trial was to be Alastair MacDonald, also of Duncan.

It was March of 1974 before Harvey had gathered enough information for his defence. He appears to have been puzzled as indicated by this letter to him from the prosecuting attorney:

MACDONALD LETTER TO HARVEY

31(317)   January 28, 1974

Messrs. Lines and Harvey
Barristers and Solicitors
127 Ingram Street
Duncan, B.C.

ATTENTION: J.G. Harvey, Esq.

Dear Sirs:

                    Re: Regina V. Douglas Holman
                         Section 4, Wildlife Act

        Further to our telephone conversation, I now under-
stand that Mrs. Rustulka delivered to you a copy of the
information.

        The particulars are that on the evening of
November 21 last Conservation Officer Gosling attended
at the residence of the Accused and advised the Accused
he was investigating a report that a radio-collared
cougar had been shot and he had reason to believe that
the Accused had done the shooting. The accused denied
all knowledge of this and gratuitously said that he
had not in fact killed a cougar for years. On request
the Accused produced a valid hunting license on the
reverse of which showed that the Accused had purchased
a deer tag. On being further questioned, the Accused
advised that he had not purchased any other tags.
*After some 25 minutes to half an hour the matter of a radio-
collared cougar was again raised and the Accused advised
Mr. Gosling that if he heard anything about it he would let the
Department know.* Mr. Gosling again emphasized that
they were most anxious to recover the collar as it was
an important portion of data in a cougar movement
study. The Conservation Officer then left.

        Having regard to the rule in the Peche case there
will, of course, on trial have to be a Voir Dire concerning this conversation. As there were others
present whose names are unknown to the Crown, I would
appreciate being advised as to who these parties are in
order that they may be called.

145

Macdonald letter to Harvey (continued).

Further investigation revealed that a cougar had been killed, that this cougar had "something around its neck", that the cougar in question was suspected of killing the sheep owned by the informant.

As a result of this conversation, the Officer then attended upon one Walker and Walker was advised of the purpose of the visit. Walker then said that he, your client and his nephew went hunting a cougar. After a short chase, Walker's dogs treed the cougar. While it was up the tree, Walker observed it to be wearing some sort of a collar and he made a comment that perhaps it should not be shot. Your client shot the cougar, dragged it out to a vehicle, and your client took it home.

On the evening of November 22, Conservation Officer Gosling again attended at the Accused's residence and advised the Accused that he had received information which implicated the Accused in the killing of a cougar. Holman was asked if he wished to change his story and he replied in the affirmative. He further stated that on the previous evening he was afraid to tell the truth because he had destroyed the collar. He admitted taking the dead animal home and skinning it and said the hide was rubbed from the collar being around its neck and that this rubbing made the hide unsuitable for tanning, so the hide, the collar and ear tags were burned.

This charge arose as a result of the investigation.

Yours very truly,

AIM:dk

copy to Department of Recreation and Conservation
        Fish and Wildlife Branch
        Provincial Building
        Duncan, B.C.

        ATTENTION: G. Gosling, Esq.

(Italics are ours)

The trial in Duncan on March 5 was well attended. Farming was a way of life. Government procedure only got in the way.

Here is a copy of the proceedings:

CRIME REPORT

▶→ QUADRUPLICATE TO CONSERVATION OFFICER ◀—◀

BRITISH COLUMBIA FISH AND WILDLIFE BRANCH

CRIME REPORT

REGION Vancouver Island   DATE March 6/74   FILE No. 19-02

DETACHMENT Duncan

P.C.R. | REGINA vs.

HOLMAN, Douglas George
COMPLETE NAME

Mt. Sicker Road, Westholme, B.C.
COMPLETE ADDRESS

CHARGE Douglas George HOLMAN, between October 1st A.D. 1973 and October 31st A.D. 1973, at or near Westholme in the Province of British Columbia, unlawfully did hunt wildlife, to wit: cougar, at a time not within the open season, contrary to form of statute in such case made and provided.

SECTION OF ACT Sect. 4 (1) (c) Wildlife Act   DATE CHARGE LAID Nov. 26th, 1973

HEARING

CHARGE LAID BY Gordon D. Gosling, Conservation Officer   DATE March 5/74

PLACE Duncan

MAGISTRATE Judge Lance Heard   PLEA

APPEARANCES: FOR PROSECUTION Al MacDonald   Not guilty

FOR DEFENCE Mr. Harvey

ADJUDICATION

Found Guilty   RECEIPT No.

DISPOSITION OF FINE AND COSTS OR PRISONER IF GADL SENTENCE

SIGNED BY: _____   POSITION Conservation Officer

This space for evidence if plea not guilty; disposition of any licence or permit, action taken; remarks, etc. If insufficient space attach separate plain sheet.

The circumstances leading up to the above charge were covered in a report to you dated Nov. 23/73, file No. 61-06.

Judge Heard has reserved his decision as to penalty until a later date. That date may be after I have moved to Prince George. Therefore I am submitting this Crime Report without the penalty. Al MacDonald will eventually cover the penalty in his report to Mr. Estlin.

EXAMINED AND FORWARDED TO FISH AND WILDLIFE BRANCH. VICTORIA.   19___

SIGNED BY: SUPERVISOR.

The trial made the front page of the *Cowichan Leader* and in the March 7 issue the editor devoted four columns to the proceedings.

Court Decision Reserved On
Holman Cougar Shooting

Judge Lance Heard reserved a decision Tuesday in provincial court on the case of Douglas Holman of Westholme who pleaded not guilty to a charge of shooting a cougar out of season.

The case arose out of an incident at the H. V. Mabley farm in Westholme last October where a male cougar which had killed a sheep was cornered and shot.

The cougar which was shot had been tagged and a radio collar put around his neck to track him.

Thomas (Sandy) Walker appearing for the prosecution told the court that Mabley had found one of his sheep mauled in the yard and had asked him "if Walker could bring his dogs over and see if there was a cougar or wild dog in the area."

Walker then went to the accused and asked him if he would come along and see why the sheep had died. Holman then went with Walker to the Mabley residence where they inspected the sheep.

Walker said that Holman and himself decided that a cougar had killed the sheep and the Mableys then asked the two men if they could find the cougar and destroy it. The men agreed to this and Walker set his dogs off to track the cat and Holman was given Walker's rifle to use to shoot it when found.

"The dogs soon caught the scent and chased the cougar up a tree," Walker said.

"Holman then came along and shot the cougar and put it in a truck and took it home and that is the last I saw of it," Walker said.

Game Warden Gordon Gosling told the court that he had been informed of the incident about a month later and subsequently investigated the incident.

He said that he understood the cougar wore a radio collar used for tracking certain cats in the woods and also that he had been tagged.

The main reason for his investigation said Gosling was to try to return the collar and tags to the department which was carrying on the studies.

"I paid two visits to Holman at his home," Gosling said, "to just ask him what had happened to the collar and tags and did not at that time have any intention of charging him with any wrong doing.

"On my first visit in late November Holman said that he hadn't even shot a cougar for years and didn't know anything about the incident in question.

"I then went back to investigate a little more and returned to the Holman residence the next evening at which time Holman admitted the incident took place but that he was afraid to tell the night before because of what might happen."

Gosling said Holman told that he had burned the carcass of the cougar and the collar and tags with it because the cougar was in a very unhealthy state.

Crown Prosecutor Alastair MacDonald then called Percy Dewar to the stand who testified about the collar and tags which he had placed on the animal in July 1973.

Dewar described the collar and the tracking of the cougar for the first weeks after it was wired.

He said the equipment on the animal was valued about $100 and the department with which he was working on this project would like to have the tags and collar back.

MacDonald then rested the Crown's case.

Defence counsel Godfrey Harvey proceeded to try to show that Holman was doing the shooting of the animal for the protection of domestic animals.

Harvey argued that Holman had been asked to shoot the animal without reward or gain and that Holman was innocent under the Sheep Protection Act which says a person may shoot a dog that is killing sheep on private property and also the section in the Wildlife Act that states a person may kill an animal on his land which is endangering or killing domestic animals.

Holman took the stand and said that he thought Gosling meant, "had I shot a cougar in the last couple of weeks. I didn't think he was talking about the one I'd shot over a month ago," Holman said.

Holman then admitted shooting the cougar in question but said he didn't think he was breaking the law by doing so as someone had asked him to shoot it as a favour as it was on private property.

He insisted that he had burned the hide and with it the collar and

149

tags because they had no address of where to return them and he didn't know what they were for.

Mrs. Mabley, a defence witness, then stated that her husband had asked Walker to come and inspect his sheep and consequently Holman shot the cougar.

She said Gosling had told her that no charges would be laid against Holman for doing the shooting but that they just wanted the return of the collar and tags.

Under cross examination Mrs. Mabley admitted that she had not specifically asked Holman to shoot the cougar and she hadn't heard her husband ask him either.

The defence rested its case with Godfrey Harvey saying that, in the interest of the public, Holman should be acquitted.

"There were several young children in the area," he pleaded, "who had to be protected and any man would have done what Holman had done. If you can kill a dog who is destroying your animals then you should be able to kill a cougar."

Judge Heard said in answer to defence arguments that,

"Holman was the wrong person to do the killing and the Sheep Protection Act only covers dogs."

Judge Heard said he was reserving a decision until March 12 to try to find out about the collar and tags as he felt the case depended largely on the safe return of these.

The *Cowichan Leader* followed the reaction closely. Involved were many facets, the Fish & Wildlife Branch, farmers, hunters, conservationists, bleeding hearts plus many a curious onlooker. Letters-to-the-Editor flooded in. The most controversial, perhaps, was from Penny Dewar and printed in the March 14 edition:

Editor:

Your newspaper recently printed an article on a court case in Duncan in which Douglas Holman was on trial for shooting a cougar during a closed season.

I was present at that case and realize that some very misleading information was brought out in court.

After fitting the cougar with a radio collar my sister and I spent several weeks following him very closely during day and night.

If Mr. Holman's statement was true about the cougar "coming down to kill sheep" then he would have been living off sheep from the day that we first followed him.

That cougar lived continuously close to farms, feeding on deer which otherwise could have proven troublesome to the farmers.

Many times we followed him close to sheep and other livestock and he never bothered them.

I cannot explain why this cougar did eventually kill a sheep but perhaps if Mr. Holman had reported that he shot the cougar to the Fish and Wildlife Branch, then we might have been able to find this out.

I would not trust Mr. Holman's observations as anyone who thinks that a cougar holds a two-week food supply in its stomach knows very little about these animals.

I also doubt Mr. Holman's statement that the radio collar had rubbed the hair off the cougar's neck. That collar had been on for less than four months when the cougar was shot.

We have recently changed the collars on two cougars that had been wearing collars for over a year and the collars had in no way affected the hide on their necks.

I might add that the plastic ear tags that we put on the cougars are the same as those used successfully on cattle.

A cougar wearing a radio collar and ear tags was recently shot north of Campbell River.

This animal was taken as a trophy animal and the collar and ear tags were promptly turned over to the Fish and Wildlife Branch.

Mr. Holman's failure to do this merely points out his ignorance of the B.C. Hunting Regulations which state clearly "Report any tagged bird or animal to the Fish and Wildlife Branch."

As Mr. Holman and Mr. Walker are cougar hunters one would think that they would have been most interested in helping our study.

We have had considerable publicity in newspapers and magazines and I doubt whether they could have been ignorant of our work.

The last time that we were able to track the cougar they shot was in August, 1973.

However, we continued trying to find him, both from the ground and air, until long after his death. If these men had reported when they shot the cougar, then much wasted time and money would have been saved.

I was very disappointed to hear Mr. Holman's lawyer, Mr. Harvey, state that the cougar "not only a menace to sheep but also to human life."

This is a ridiculous statement that puts needless fear into people. The number of attacks by cougars on humans is so small that it should never be considered.

We have followed radio-collared cougars that have approached people in the woods picking salal, and, when the cougars realized that humans were near, they ran away from them.

I should add that we were following them from a distance that we knew would not disturb them. We have also had four different cougars come within 100 yards of our camp and all of them just walked by.

I am not denying the fact that cougars have attacked people, however I am saying that it is ridiculous to assume that every cougar that is seen is going to attack.

There are so few such incidents that one must think that they were caused by some strange occurrence such as a cougar being sick or wounded. The incidents with a cougar two summers ago in Strathcona Park were preceded by the wounding of a cougar in the same area by a man with a .22 rifle. That cougar had been harmless until it was wounded.

Penny Dewar

Perhaps Mrs. Dewar underestimated the power of the press. In any case, her letter brought a storm of protest as evinced by more letters to the *Cowichan Leader*.

Doug Holman's reply:

Editor:

First I would like to get a few things straight about the remarks made about me by Mrs. Penny Dewar with regards to the cougar I shot in Westholme.

Why she has informed the public about the facts regarding the cougar I shot in Westholme, are misleading, is unknown but could it possibly be that they are too biased to reason with facts and are afraid of losing any further grants when such proof is brought forward?

She also doubted my statement that the hair on the cougar's neck was rubbed and the ears were infected. It is too bad that I had destroyed this evidence and if I knew it was going to go this far, I definitely would have taken the hide to the S.P.C.A. for examination. I am not against research of this kind but when they ignore facts one wonders what kind of research they are doing.

The government has already given them grants, they say they spent $15,000 of their own money and are now asking for a further $35,000. With all this money spent what have they accomplished?

They have learned that there are approximately 25 cougars in their research area, that a female cougar does not travel very far and a male has no limits to his travel. This is a great amount of money spent to learn so little and I feel that this money should be spent on wiser things such as saving elk and deer.

Percy Dewar should recall when his brother Jim had killed a cougar after it had killed a small Indian boy on the West Coast and also the fellow who was pulled out of his sleeping bag by another.

A previous letter from B. Dixon stating he had shot 17 on his farm near the research area after each cougar was caught killing his livestock. There are, no doubt, many more incidents of this nature that we have not heard of or have since forgotten.

In my lifetime of hunting cougars I have personally killed at least 40 cougars that have been killing sheep and know of many more.

Mrs. Dewar now states that the number of attacks by cougars on humans is so small that it should NEVER be considered. Why should she care as it probably won't be her child that might be mauled or killed as she figures her cougars are more important than your children or livestock.

She also states she was AMAZED at how close they followed cougars to where people lived and they didn't even know about it. Maybe it amazes her also when these cougars kill your livestock.

She has been affiliated with cougar studies for only a couple of years and apparently feels she knows more about cougar life than local hunters with years of experience.

Mrs. Dewar states that usually only a young cougar kills livestock as he was never really taught what to kill. This is also misleading as the cougar I just shot was at least five years old and I cannot recall killing any young cougar that had killed cattle or sheep.

I am sure other hunters will tell you the same thing. He said he would also like to see the selling of cougar pelts abolished and yet he used to kill them for money himself. Who knows maybe he will get all these cougars lined up and then suddenly once again turn guide and make a pocket full killing them, anything is possible as it didn't take him long to change from cat killer to cat lover.

In my opinion this all boils down to a couple of things. One is that they could care less if someone is hurt by a cougar or if your livestock are killed.

Two, that they ignore facts and third, that the grants they are getting from different sources are going to waste as it seems they are accomplishing very little.

Doug Holman

Doug was not the only person riled enough to protest.

E. S. Marrs, a keen conservationist, farmer and logger penned some spicy answers. His letter also appeared, next to Doug's, in the March 21 issue:

Editor:

In reply to the letter by Mrs. P. Dewar in your March 14 issue, I would state that the Holman family is a highly respected family in this area, that they have many times gone to the aid of farmers without thought of remuneration and that even if Mrs. Dewar does not trust Mr. Holman's observations—we would rather trust his gun in our flock of sheep than one of Mrs. Dewar's collared pussy cats!

Perhaps Mrs. Dewar's idea that the number of attacks on humans is small, is just, so far, a matter of luck.

We had a cougar troubling us here some years ago that was definitely a menace, indeed that children could not go out of the yard for sometime on the advice of James Dewar, a provincial predatory hunter and I might add an equally helpful man to the farmer.

Why did that cougar kill the sheep? Why did a cougar kill seven of our lambs, batter two ewes to insensibility and eat one head of one lamb?

Perhaps Mrs. Dewar, who seems to have so many answers and so great an antipathy to good, decent cougar hunters, (who are the

154

farmers' friend) should read two books from the Vancouver Island Regional Library—*Leemo* and *More About Leemo* by Stanley Brock. Perhaps if she reads these books she could stop all her expensive studies, since it's all been done before, and stop her blathering! Perhaps we'd all be happier without it.

In closing, may I add a farmer's deep appreciation to all of the fine cougar hunters, who have come to our aid over the years, when sheep-killing cougar have bothered us.

E. S. Marrs

A biting reply to Mrs. Dewar's letter, titled *Matter of Luck*, got second billing next to the Marrs' letter. Magnus Colvin, Sr., respected as a top-rate logger, bridge builder and woodsman on Vancouver Island wrote:

Editor:

In your last issue a correspondent writes, under the heading; "Cougar Case Misleading" "If Mr. Holman's statement was true about the cougar coming down to kill sheep then he would be living off sheep from the day we first followed him."

This does not necessarily follow. The cougar had been living on deer which are in poor condition. The does are with fawn and the bucks are not in velvet. I know! The cougar needed a change of diet, a little fat.

"A cougar was recently shot north of Campbell River. This was a 'Trophy Animal'," she said. When is the "trophy season"?

"I was very disappointed to hear Mr. Holman's lawyer, Mr. Harvey, state that the cougar . . . not only a menace to sheep but also to human life."

"This is a ridiculous statement," the writer said.

This is not a ridiculous statement, but a fact. I know, I was born here 80 years ago and the cougars killed many of our sheep. I can remember one ewe which had triplets which a cougar killed one night not over 100 feet from the kitchen door. In the morning we found the three lambs huddled near the carcass.

"And puts needless fear into people. The number of attacks on humans is so small that it should never be considered," she continued:

155

This is a most astounding statement. A young girl of 12 (Ashburnham) beat off a large male cougar which had attacked her young brother at Cowichan Lake, vie *Cowichan Leader* (1915?).

A large male cougar chased head rigger Bill Numi out of the woods with the rest of the crew to the skidder donkey at VLM Co. claim Cowichan Lake camp 10. The donkey engineer drove him off with scalding water from the steam hose. I was there, 1935.

A female cougar entered a logging camp in daylight and attacked a woman at Nimkish not too long ago. One of the loggers wrestled with the beast with no other weapons except his two hands. No holds barred. Catch as catch can. Greco and Lancaster. Needless to say, he won the match. However, the unfortunate woman was badly mauled and spent several months in the hospital but your correspondent states "this is so small that it should never be considered."

Not so long ago a young girl was attacked by a cougar near Calgary. Fortunately the mother was able to drive it away but not before the girl was a serious hospital case.

A man was attacked near Campbell River not so long ago while in his tent camp.

While I was working Fairbridge farm (1935) a young male cougar killed six sheep one night. He merely lapped the blood and ate the livers. The scene resembles an action of a cat playing with a lot of mice. Mr. Lee Berrow was soon on the site and turned up with a young male. The cougars, in my opinion, like a change of diet. When one has been eating apples for a long time then pears look enticing.

Magnus Colvin, Sr.

This was too much for Percy Dewar, Penny's husband. Pleading for understanding, he wrote:

Editor:

This is another letter from a houndsman. Answering Mr. Watt's letter, concerning the cougar study, yet it is a family affair. He spoke of dedication, my sister-in-law, Susan Brown has worked with us on this study for over one year without being paid. This type of dedicated person is very hard to find.

We are aware of all of the studies being done in the U.S.A. on cougars. We have corresponded several times with Dr. Maurice

156

Hornocker who has been studying cougars in Idaho since 1964.

Three biologists—James Monteith from California, Harley Shaw from Arizona and Richard Poelker from Washington (who is presently staying with us) have come here to visit us and learn our techniques prior to commencing studies on cougars in their respective states.

These people are presently working with the full co-operation of the houndsmen in their areas.

As a Canadian I feel that I would rather try to learn about our wildlife than to be told facts which may not apply here by our American neighbours.

Several times we have asked fellow houndsmen to contribute to us their knowledge on cougars. Once again we ask for this co-operation.

Instead of criticizing our work when you are completely unaware of the facts, we ask you to come to us with the vast amount of information which we know you must have. I will add that anyone who feels that we are harming the cougars that we work on is cordially invited to come out with us to see our work in person.

Regarding money, my wife has already mentioned that we never received $35,000 and that we have never spent 5 cents of taxpayers' money.

As for the $15,000 that we have spent in the last two years, a considerable amount of it was spent searching for the cougar in question.

Mr. Watt (related to the Holman's, ed.) recently admitted to me that he had seen the cougar wearing the radio collar shortly after it was shot and he failed to report his knowledge of this collar to the Fish and Wildlife Branch as the hunting regulations state that he should.

I feel that my wife and I are qualified to do this study as we have both been long associated with the outdoors of Vancouver Island.

My brother Jim Dewar, a well-known hunter, was a predator hunter for the Fish and Wildlife Branch for 30 years.

I have earned the biggest part of my living during the last 30 years from hunting. My wife's grandmother, one of the Cliffe's, a well-known outdoor family, was born in the Comox Valley in 1885 and her grandfather, Joe Thomson came to Vancouver Island at the age of 20 in 1894 and spent all of his life in the outdoors on this island and a big part of it as a timber cruiser.

He was a close observer of wildlife and before he died at 94 he had passed on much of his knowledge. Since we began this study my wife has spent more time hunting cougars than many houndsmen will in their lifetime.

Neither my wife nor I have at any time condemned anyone for killing a cougar that was killing livestock, nor have we ever criticized anyone for spending their time and money as they saw fit.

It is beyond my understanding that people are so ready to condone a man who destroyed valuable public property. I have much sympathy for Mr. Mabley for the loss of his ewe but I cannot understand why so few people feel the same for us concerning our loss.

As a warning to other hunters, my reward for helping a friend by killing a cougar on his sheep farm was the uncalled for letter from Mr. Marrs which contained nasty and personal remarks about the work we are doing.

Percy Dewar

Unfortunately for Percy and Penny Dewar they didn't get in the last word. This went to H. Bradshaw, whose letter appeared alongside Percy's in the April 11 edition of the *Cowichan Leader*. Bradshaw commanded attention, not only as an astute outdoorsman, keeper of hounds and cougar hunter but as a farmer, truck logger and old-time resident.

His tongue-in-cheek remarks keep the reader glued to the page:

Editor:

This is in reply to Mrs. Dewar's letter in the March 28 edition of the *Cowichan Leader* where she is so intent on running Mr. Holman down for shooting a sheep-killing cougar that had a radio collar on.

I wonder if it ever occurred to Mrs. Dewar that it is quite a loss to farmers to have their livestock killed as they are trying to be independent and make their own living not relying on the tax payer for grants or welfare.

In previous articles Mrs. Dewar makes a great thing about living in a plastic covered dwelling that is only a short distance from the highway. Is she trying to impress people that you have to live this way to hunt cougar or is it because we have a new element of people in our society who live this way and have no trouble getting grants and welfare?

Mrs. Dewar states that they have spent $15,000 of their own money. This is a terrible waste because if they had gone to see Mr. Dick Clark of Hilliers who has hunted the Northwest Bay area for over 60 years, and no doubt has killed more cougars than anyone on Vancouver Island he could have in a few hours told them more about cougars than they have learned in their two-year study.

Mrs. Dewar says that Mr. Holman doubts her husband's word that most of the cougars killing livestock are young males. Maybe if she got in touch with the people that have lost their animals she would find out that at least three quarters of these cougars have been adults.

Mrs. Dewar states that all that is available to the public is childish literature. I suppose she will say the same about the study made in Idaho by M. G. Hornocker and hunter Wilber Wiles with his two good dogs. There is a very good article about it in the *National Geographic Magazine* November 1969.

She also says Mr. Marrs has a short memory as Percy. Dewar was at his place four times when cougars were killing his sheep. This first time he got a cougar that had been seen lying on the road. The other times the late Jim Dewar had been called in his capacity of government hunter and usually did a good job.

Later Percy Dewar arrived and he had a client with him and his biggest concern was to get a trophy for his hunter, but with no luck. However while there, he was told of a cougar being seen on Mr. Marrs' driveway. After being taken to the spot, within about twenty minutes, the famous Blue Tick hounds were turned loose on the track, there was a lot of barking and howling but no cougar treed. The client finally asked Mr. Marrs if he could have an old hide that was hanging in the shed as he didn't want to go back East without a hide. So much for the expert with forty years' experience.

In a statement made over the radio Mrs. Dewar says that if a cougar kills a sheep it won't come back and kill anymore as it doesn't like the wool. For Mrs. Dewar's information the only way most cougars stop killing sheep is when they are killed (themselves).

Another thing her husband with his forty years' experience

159

didn't tell her or didn't know is that a cougar doesn't eat the wool but can roll the hide off a sheep better than a lot of humans can.

I think it is about time that Mrs. Dewar apologized to Mr. Holman and kept her nose out of other peoples' affairs.

There is also little doubt that by the time they have finished their study Mr. Holman will have forgotten more about cougar and hunting than they will ever know.

H. Bradshaw

Judge Heard announced his reserved decision on March 12, one week after the trial. He found Doug Holman guilty as charged and imposed a fine, thus starting one of the longest and bitterest protests the B.C. Game Department had ever encountered. Phones buzzed, office typewriters clattered, and the moccasin telegraph went full speed. What had begun as no more than a routine neighbourly favour in the small area of Westholme ballooned to a furore over all of Vancouver Island and most of the Gulf Islands.

Game Commissioner Dr. James Hatter hastily called a public meeting for March 24 at the Commercial Hotel to try and smooth things out. An overflow crowd turned up at Duncan that Sunday afternoon. There were farmers, sportsmen, lawyers and businessmen from all parts of Vancouver Island. Sheep rancher and cougar hunter Bob Akerman brought a group from Saltspring Island to protest Doug's prosecution and conviction. The crowd was generally in agreement with Bob.

If this, they decided, was the way the game laws worked, then changes were in order. Many speakers commended Doug for his actions and good neighbourly common sense. The meeting ended with motion to request the government to revise and clarify the Game Act.

Bob Akerman moved: "When a dangerous predator has killed domestic stock or is endangering human life, then permits, tags or other impediments should be done away with until the animal is dispatched."

This motion was seconded and carried without one dissenting vote.

Dolph Holman (Doug's brother) and I called Dr. Hatter and his assistant Don Robinson aside and advised them that we were planning to have Doug's conviction appealed. They both thought this would be a good idea and promised advice and assistance. We told them we had contacted Bob Hutchison of Crease & Company, Barristers & Solicitors, Victoria, to act on the appeal.

"Is that the son of Bruce Hutchison, the author?" asked Don Robinson.

"That's right," Dolph answered, and added, "He's also a top-notch Steelheader."

"Yes, we know him," Dr. Hatter put in. "He's a smart young lawyer and a great conservationist. Just tell him to come to our office and we'll give him all the help we can."

"Most people here think Doug should have got a medal, not a fine," I advised them.

"Case should never have reached the courts," was Dr. Hatter's observation.

We phoned Hutch (Bob Hutchison) and invited him to meet us at our favourite fishing hole at daylight the next Monday morning.

"Hell, I'm not like you," he laughed. "I've got to be in the office by ten o'clock tomorrow."

"If you meet us at the Big Hole at five o'clock we'll guarantee you your limit by eight a.m.," I assured him. "That gives you two hours to drive back to Victoria."

"Tell him I've got plenty of good bait," Dolph urged.

"I heard that," Hutch laughed. "Ten to five on Monday. I'll be there."

True to his word, Hutch turned up on time. We had six

161

nice Steelhead beached by 7:30. One doe was close to 16 pounds. Whenever we weren't playing a fish we would explain Doug's situation as best we could.

Bob was happy to help us. He promised to have the appeal heard as soon as possible. He wrote down the two lawyers' names and phone numbers.

"How much do you think it will cost?" asked Dolph.

"Two hundred if we are lucky, not more than three in any case," he replied.

"How about a good side of Hereford beef for your locker instead of cash?" I suggested. Dolph and I were raising registered Herefords.

"You can pick your own animal when you are ready. They're averaging about $285 to the side right now," Dolph said casually.

With a broad smile, Bob shook hands with both of us and said, "It's a deal. I'll be up next Saturday. We can fish a bit and then pick the beef. I'll need to talk to Doug for a few minutes. Why not bring him fishing?"

Saturday morning we got a few nice fish and Bob picked his beef at Dolph's place and had a chat with Doug. Everything seemed to be going well.

"Should be in court in about three weeks' time," Bob announced as he left for home.

"Beef will be ready about that time," Dolph assured him.

So much for best-laid plans. Two weeks later I received a frantic phone call from Bob who said, "Appeal is set down for eleven next Monday morning. Now get this. When I called Doug to make sure he could be there he flatly refused. He said, 'I'm not going through all that again,' and hung up the phone. Now he won't answer my calls. Do you think you could persuade him to appear? There are 99 chances out of a hundred we'll win!"

"I'll leave right now, Bob, and do what I can."

"Tell him I've spent a lot of time getting all the arrangements made. The way it looks to me right now, he will get his fine back and only be in court for a very short time. Let Doug know this."

"I'll explain it to Doug and call you back."

Arriving at Westholme I found Doug at his younger brother's house. He and Fred were looking at a big salmon in the back of Doug's pickup. Glancing up, Doug asked proudly, "What do you think of that baby?"

Hefting the salmon with both hands, I took a calculated guess, "Twenty-eight pounds?"

"Thirty-two!" Fred bragged, with a broad grin.

After some fish talk I carefully broached the subject of the appeal trial. The smile left Doug's face. He became very serious.

I was disappointed and puzzled, so I said, "Hutch is waiting for your answer right now about Monday morning. What shall I tell him?"

"Tell him there are too many people involved. Can't drag them through all that again. I never shot that sick cougar. I told someone else to do it and I've had to pay the price. Leave it that way," and he got into his pickup and drove away without even a good-bye.

Fred kicked a piece of bark from his driveway, shook his head, looked me in the eye and said grimly, "That's the end of that. Too bad."

"Might as well call Hutch from here so's he can get proceedings cancelled," I suggested.

It had to be done. I got Hutch on the line and delivered the bad news and he replied, "Damn shame. We had things cinched to clear him in every way."

"Pick up your beef at Dolph's place at noon Saturday, Hutch. It's ready and we can talk then."

Next morning Hutch was quiet as the beef was loaded. His

163

disappointment matched ours. He glanced at Dolph and myself, "Don't feel like I've earned this. How about if I pay you for it?"

"Not your fault," Dolph replied bluntly. "You did your part. Not your fault Doug changed his mind."

So ended the affair of the collared cougar. Yet, there are unexplained factors.

Why was Gosling transferred to Prince George after the conviction? Why was there no evidence produced to involve Doug's nephew? Danger to the Mabley children not stressed?

We remind you of the trial report in the *Cowichan Leader*: Judge Heard said in answer to defence arguments that,

"Holman was the wrong person to do the killing and the Sheep Protection Act ONLY COVERS DOGS."

*　　*　　*

Further your attention is directed to the following excerpts from official documents of more recent times.

Fourth Session, Thirty-second Parliament
30-31 Elizabeth II, 1981-82
Legislative Assembly of British Columbia

Bill 55
WILDLIFE ACT
(page 26, section 76)

A person who kills or wounds big game or an animal of an endangered or threatened species by accident or kills or wounds big game for the protection of life or property and fails to report the killing or wounding and the location of that wildlife promptly to an officer, commits an offence.

BRITISH COLUMBIA HUNTING REGULATION SYNOPSIS
1984-85
(page 3, column 2)

IT IS UNLAWFUL
- to make...
- to hunt wildlife at any time during the year except within the open season or by authority of a permit issued under the Wildlife Act.

Bill 55 is not readily accessible to the average person.

If anyone should be caught between a mother cougar and her kittens it is unlikely there would be sufficient time to fill out the necessary forms and get a permit.

From Island to Island

We had been trying to put all the pieces together about the shooting of a collared cougar at Westholme on Vancouver Island.

Doug Holman had been prosecuted and the trial caused a nasty uproar. There were rumours floating around about this same cougar killing livestock in the Burgoyne Valley on Saltspring Island. We weren't getting enough facts to be sure.

I decided to call Bob Akerman. He was the man who shot or kept track of most cougars when and if they swam from Vancouver Island across the Sansum Narrows.

When he came to the phone, I asked, "Bob, are you going to be home tomorrow?"

"We should be here all day. Are you planning to come over?" he invited.

"Yes, I'd like to have a chat with you and son Ted about the cougar that caused so much trouble over there the summer of 1973. We could catch the early ferry from

Crofton to Vesuvius and be at your place about eight-thirty if that's okay with you," I suggested.

"Sounds great. I'll ask Ted to come down. Between the two of us, we can probably dig up what you need to know."

We were about halfway to Vesuvius on the seven-thirty ferry. The morning was warm with a pleasant breeze blowing up the channel from the south. Using binoculars, we could clearly see the two points where the Sansum Narrows close in to less than a half a mile wide.

"That's the place where the cougars usually swim across," I pointed out to Ruby.

"Has anyone seen them doing it?" she asked.

"The Maxwell family lived there since the 1870's. Tom and I were along when Old Dick Maxwell told Dad how he had seen one swimming in the narrows. Dick was out fishing for salmon and was almost over to the Vancouver Island side when this thing swam by. He thought it was just a big seal at first, but when it didn't go under like seals do, he got curious and followed it.

"When the thing walked up on the beach, he saw the long tail and realized he had been following a cougar. It shook itself several times, then climbed up on some rocks and began licking its wet fur. Besides this one, there were several other cougars spotted swimming from Vancouver Island to Saltspring. This is an old-time cougar crossing.

"Those mountains are plenty steep on both sides of the narrows. Trees, lots of brush and some open bluffs make it ideal country for cougars to hang around in."

When we arrived at the Akermans', Molly had coffee made and Bob had dug out all sorts of notes, pictures, and old newspaper clippings.

"Ted can't be here until around ten-thirty," Bob told us.

"Well, Bob, how about you telling us about your grandparents while we are waiting for Ted? It would be interesting

167

to hear what it was like from the 1860's on," I suggested.

Bob had boxes of papers and pictures his father had kept. "I'll start at the beginning," he said. "Where the parliament buildings now stand in Victoria, my grandfather, Joe, had a market garden. He farmed there from the late 1850's on into the 1860's. In the fall of 1859 he rowed up to this valley for a hunting trip with some friends.

"In those days, there were both elk and bear on Salt-spring. Deer and grouse were so plentiful, it wasn't much of a challenge to get all you wanted. The creek down there," Bob said, pointing out the window, "was teeming with salmon.

"Grandpa Joe was a born farmer. When he saw the fertile soil along the creek banks, he decided then and there he wanted land here. He filed pre-emption papers for 160 acres as soon as he got back to Victoria. For the next few years, he kept his gardens going in Victoria during the summers, but winters were spent here, clearing land and building a log cabin.

"My grandmother landed in Victoria on the *Robert Lowe*, January 1, 1863. This was the famous brideship that brought some thirty-six young ladies from the British Isles to Victoria. Like others, Grandpa Joe must have decided he needed some help and company to go along with his pioneering plans. There were over a hundred young bachelors waiting on the dock when the brideship tied up.

"Grandpa wasted no time in courting and proposing marriage to Martha Clay.

"After a short honeymoon spent here in the valley, they went back to live in Victoria until their first baby, Frannie, was born on November 22, 1865. It wasn't long after Frannie came along that the young couple sold their property in Victoria and got ready for the trek to Saltspring.

"In early February, they hauled all their belongings from

168

The three Clay sisters sailed around Cape Horn from England in the bride ship *Robert Lowe* to land in Victoria, British Columbia, January 1, 1863. Standing; Emma (Mrs. Rourk). Sitting, left; Martha (Mrs. Joe Akerman), born March 16, 1835. Right: Fannie (Mrs. Stevenson). Martha is Bob Akerman's grandmother.

"How many times do I have to tell you kids—first your homework, and THEN you can have fun...!"

BOB BIERMAN—VICTORIA DAILY TIMES

November 23, 1965. Young Paddy Akerman, 10, of Saltspring Island, B.C. (left) holds rifle he used to fell a male cougar near his home on Sunday. Paddy was with his father and brother Doug, 13, and cousin Bruce Benton, 16 (right), shown with three cats shot that week by the Akermans. All were males and theory is they were enticed to Saltspring from Vancouver Island by mating calls of a female cougar.

Ted Akerman shot this cougar near his home. It had killed the six sheep in a fenced pasture the night before. This happened in 1973 near the bottom of Lee's hill going into Burgoyne Valley on south Saltspring Island.

the Saanich Peninsula to the beach where the creek runs into Fulford Harbour. Grandpa hired Indians with canoes to paddle this seven miles and then help pack up to the cabin. They brought with them all sorts of vegetable seeds, fruit trees, some chickens, and all sorts of other things, including a dog and some roses.

"There were no roads, no wharf, no land surveyed, no post office and no stores of any kind. They were the first white family to take up land and become permanent settlers. All supplies had to be brought in by rowboat or Indian canoes.

"They almost lost their baby to a big tom cougar the first year they were here," Bob continued. "Grandma was hoeing the garden when she looked up to see this huge animal pawing her baby and sniffing at its face. This was only ten feet away from the cabin door. She let out a scream and charged the prowler, waving her hoe in its face, 'Get out! Get out or I'll kill you!' she screamed. The cougar backed away, snarling and swiping at the hoe with his big paws. When it jumped into the bushes back of the cabin, she grabbed the baby and ran inside to bar the door.

"Grandpa Joe was away on a job. When he got home and Grandma told him about her scare, Grandpa just shrugged and said he would take care of the problem if she would just get some supper ready. He shot and had the devil's skin stretched on the back wall of their cabin before dark that evening.

"The hide measured just over nine feet from the nose to the tip of its tail. The records show this to be the largest cougar ever shot on Saltspring.

"In April of 1868," Bob continued, "Uncle Joe was born. The first white child on Saltspring. Next came two girls, Matilda and Martha."

"When was your dad born, Bob?" I asked.

169

Bob ruffled his papers, then replied "On December 28th, 1873. He was christened George Edward but was always known as Ted.

"As young men, Uncle Joe and Dad became road foremen and were responsible for the original construction of most of the roads on this island. Uncle Joe handled everything from the top of the Divide Mountain north while Dad looked after everything south, including wharves and bridges.

"My Dad always had a hand in local affairs, seemed to like responsibility. He was, at one time, Chairman of the school board, Justice of the Peace, President of the Farmers' Institute and Superintendent of roads. On top of this load, he accepted the toughest job of all.

"He was appointed as a special magistrate to act as judge in all the land boundary disputes for the island. Most of these disputes arose between Dad's friends and sometimes neighbours. I remember Dad and Mother staying up nights until the wee hours trying to decide the best decision for the next day."

"Didn't you have other uncles, Bob?" I asked. "And how old was your dad when he married?"

"Yes, there was Jim, Tom and then William," Bob answered.

"Dad was 26 when he married Ellen Gyves. They raised a family of three girls and two boys. Molly was the eldest then came Dorothy and Tillie. Brother Jim was next. I came along on June 7, 1912 and was the youngest.

"Jim was a tough teacher when it came to sports. He taught me to box, play basketball, how to hunt and play baseball. My brother was almost four years older so I learned quickly—or else!" Bob remembered.

We heard a car stop in the driveway.

"That'll be Ted," he figured. "Now we can get down to some cougar talk."

Ted, the oldest son of their eleven children was slightly taller than his dad but had the same pleasant smile. "Heard you wanted some info on our island cougar," he said as he pulled up a chair.

"When was your worst year?" I asked.

"1964, we lost over half our lamb crop," Ted answered.

"Any reason for so many cougar being on the island that year?"

"The game department cancelled all the bounties in '57," Bob explained. "That started a steady increase in our sheep losses. We bought a trained cougar hound and shot a dozen or more of these killers in the next few years.

"From '63 on, things went from bad to worse," Ted added. "We shot five adult males in less than a month, all within a couple of miles of our main sheep pastures. Hardly a day went by that we didn't find more mangled sheep carcasses," Ted went on. "We'd heard a female doing her mating calls from around those caves below Maxwell Peak. We figured most of these males had been able to hear the invitation from over on Vancouver Island and decided to swim the Sansum Narrows to do something about it," Ted laughed.

"One of these damned suitors would not tree when we chased him with our hound," Bob explained. "We decided to phone the government predator hunter, Jim Dewar who, at that time, lived at Extension—about four miles south of Nanaimo.

"He was on the next ferry from Crofton. He drove off at Vesuvius in his pickup with four bluetick hounds in the back. We shouted a greeting and waved him to follow us. We took off up the old Cranberry Road.

"About a mile below the top of Maxwell Peak, we parked, right across from the trail where we'd lost the cougar only a couple of hours earlier.

"This devil was a ground fighter. He had put a sizeable rip in one of our hound's ears.

"Jim let his hounds out, then put leashes on the three younger ones. He asked us to follow but be ready to turn them loose. He wanted to try sorting things out with just his best hound by itself. This old tracker was bellowing up the trail in a matter of minutes. The young dogs were making weird noises and practically dragging us along," Ted explained.

"'Let'um loose! Let'um loose! That cat is right here!' Dewar yelled.

"The cougar had already turned to fight in the thicket. With all four hounds bellowing, the big cat broke out, then ran about a hundred yards to scramble up an old fir tree. When we got there, those hounds were barking full bore, jumping around and trying to climb the tree. The cougar had flattened itself about thirty feet up on the first big limb and was snarling down at the dogs.

"We figured it to be a four- or five-year-old male, mean and ready for battle. Dewar put all his dogs on leash and tied them well back from the tree, then finished the big cat with a single bullet through its heart. When he was sure the killer was dead, he let the hounds loose. They rushed in to maul the dead cougar.

"'Good experience for the young hounds,' Dewar explained.

"We invited Jim to stay with us for the night," Bob said. "When we drove in there was an urgent call from Gavin Mouat. Something had killed two of his best ewes just back of the barn. It was too late to try anything until morning.

"Jim and I, with the four dogs, were at Gavin's place before daylight next morning. It was really funny," Bob laughed, remembering the incident. The killer had been back and finished another sheep during the night.

"Gavin's first question was, 'Is it the work of a cougar or of dogs?' The three of us were looking at the dead sheep covered with frost. Jim and I told Gavin that this was the work of a cougar, but he wasn't so sure.

"'How do you know it's not dogs? Plenty of them running loose around here,' Gavin argued."

Bob laughed again before going on.

"If you knew Jimmy Dewar, you must also know he had a great sense of humour. With a deadpan expression, he looked Gavin straight in the eye. 'This is how,' Jim explained it to Gavin. 'I know a lot about cougar and quite a bit about dogs. There is no way to be absolutely positive what killed your three sheep.' Jim pointed to the big footprints showing clearly in the frost.

"'See those tracks, Gavin?' he said. 'The only thing I am positive of is this; the animal that made all those tracks you see down there, if it wasn't a cougar then it sure as hell was using cougar's feet.'

"We all laughed and Gavin left completely satisfied. Jim let the hounds out of the pickup and they took off with a roar up toward the bush.

"That cougar was up a tree and shot in less than twenty minutes. It had been watching us from behind an old log not more than a hundred yards from where we stood by the barn.

"I believe Jim was the best cougar hunter this province has ever known. It turned out this was the last time we saw him alive. He died of a heart attack a month later. During the 20 years that we called on Jim for help, never once did he refuse or complain," Bob finished a bit sadly.

"Do you believe he mellowed any before he died?"

"I got my doubts," Ted mused. "His parting words to me when he left on the afternoon ferry for Crofton that day were the same as twenty years earlier, 'The only good cougar is a dead one.'"

173

"That sounds like Jim all right. Now, can you tell me why you think the collared cougar Doug Holman shot at West-holme in '73 was the same one that gave you all the trouble over here?" I asked the Akermans.

"I'll let Ted tell you; he's the one who did most of the chasing of that bastard," Bob answered.

"I go by the way that animal acted," Ted began. "My first brush with him was at the Lacy's place just down the road from here. They phoned me to come over. Something had killed one of their goats and dragged it down in a gully. Dad was away in Vancouver, so I went alone. The goat was partly eaten and covered with some sticks and dry grass. From the big teeth marks on the goat's head and neck, I could sure as hell tell that this was a cougar's kill. I tried to get it with our dogs the next day but it was too dry for tracking. When the cougar went up over some dry rocks, the dogs gave up. This was in early September.

"A week later, Mrs. Lacy called again. Her other goat had been killed within ten feet of her house. It was dragged into the same ravine. Only the liver and heart had been eaten, she said.

"We were haying that day," Ted explained. "I told her we would be there first thing in the morning. When we arrived with our dogs, the Lacys' were a pretty scared family. The cougar had been back in the night to feed off the goat. As the devil was leaving, he had snatched their pet cat off the front porch, killed and carried it off. When we let the dogs loose, they chased the beast for over a mile, almost down to Burgoyne Bay. The dogs lost the trail in the big boulders above the Maxwell's barn. That cougar seemed to have no fear of people or houses. It ran through two fenced yards and crossed a main road.

"We were leasing all of the Maxwell farm at the time and had about 200 of our best ewes there. It wasn't long before

174

we found several dead sheep inside the fences. We put our dogs after that old cat several times, but he outsmarted the dogs at every turn," Ted said.

"Did you ever get a look at it?" I asked.

"In October, maybe. I was hunting deer and looking for sheep at the same time. I sneaked up through some boulders and suddenly came on a freshly killed lamb, still warm with blood oozing from its throat. Then a twig snapped. Whirling around, I saw part of a cougar's head looking at me from behind a big fir tree. There was blood on its face and I thought I saw something in its ear. Just as my rifle came up for a shot, that cougar disappeared behind the tree and took off. When I'd run the fifty yards to try for a shot, there was nothing. The bastard had vanished like a ghost.

"Twenty minutes later, Dad and I were back with our dogs. We chased that cougar for over two miles north, up along the west side of Saltspring. It was slow going over those steep bluffs and boulders. About a mile along the trail, we spotted some fresh blood and hair. That old tom had fought our dogs from a cave under an overhanging cliff. From here we could hear barking. We ran on, only to meet our dogs coming back. One was bleeding from a ripped shoulder. After a bit of coaxing, they turned and led us on down to a small sandy beach. Fresh cougar tracks led us right to the water's edge," Ted concluded.

"The cat took a swim. There is no doubt about that," Bob stated emphatically.

"Sure acted like it and could easily be the same animal that Doug Holman got," I agreed. "Bob, do you believe those dry cell batteries they were using on those cougar collars at North West Bay could survive two swims across the Sansum Narrows?"

"Not one chance in a thousand they would be any good after one trip, let alone two," Bob stated.

175

"All you have to do is have that kind of a battery close to the saltchuck for any length of time and it will corrode up and fall apart," Ted told us.

Just then, Molly and Ruby breezed in from their walk on the beach. "Want some tea or coffee?" Molly asked, putting on the kettle.

"Did you fellows come up with an answer about that Westholme cougar?" Ruby asked.

"We all agree; it's very likely to be one and the same animal," I assured her. "Furthermore, even the officials of the wildlife department told us at a meeting in Duncan that they thought it was the same cougar."

"That's all we can tell you about things that happened while it was here. There were some chickens and about a dozen tame geese that disappeared the same month that one was prowling the valley. We think the cougar got them, though we can't be sure," Ted concluded.

We sipped our tea, said our farewells, then had to rush to catch the last ferry at Vesuvius. As we drove onto the boat, I remembered Jim Dewar had made this same trip for the last time twenty years earlier.

Possum-Playing Cougar Attacks
Wildlife Officer

Animal control officer Dan Lay had a "once in a life" tangle with a cougar Sunday evening that he won't easily forget.

Lay responded to a routine call from the Jingle Pot Road area that a cougar was on the prowl.

The large cat was eventually chased up a tree by dogs around 8:30 p.m.

Lay, who is a crack shot, aimed a rifle at the head of the animal and fired.

The cougar dropped out of the tree and crashed to the ground.

Lay approached it, and to his surprise, the 22-kilogram cougar came to life and wrestled him to the ground, biting him on the face and side of the chest.

An assistant handed Lay a side gun and he shot the animal again, this time killing it.

The animal control officer was treated by a doctor for puncture wounds, but turned up for work Monday.

"This has never happened to him before," said regional conservation officer Doug Turner.

177

"It happened to Lay's father, who also used to be an animal control officer. It happens to most officers once during their careers," he added.

Turner believed Lay's first shot was "just off the mark slightly" and failed to kill the animal instantly.

The Fish and Wild Life branch in Nanaimo receives about 112 complaints every year about cougars, he said.

Nanaimo Daily Free Press, 1982

Jack Lay, Dan's father, had warned him about the dangers of shooting cougar in the head.

Jack and his wife Elaine have five children. Their three sons, Bob, Dan and Allen are all in the game department as animal control officers. Bob is at Kamloops, Dan at Nanaimo and Allen at Prince George. Their eldest daughter is Sharon while Cindy is the baby of the family.

Jack taught his sons when young to care for and handle cougar hounds and also taught them hunting and trapping.

"It was sometimes a bit crowded in the station wagon when we took off on a wild goose chase with four big hounds and all the kids. If it was a long trip and cold, the smells inside the car were not always pleasant," Mrs. Lay admitted.

Jack joined the game department October 1, 1955, and stayed on until October 1978. Twenty-three years service. He shot or trapped dozens of predators that were killing livestock or becoming dangerous to people.

We explored some of his more serious experiences with a tape recorder!

"The one on the Coquihalla River a few miles up from Hope was the most unusual experience I have ever had. It was in November and there was a foot of fresh snow. A couple of local hunters were out to get a deer. Most of the snow had already been plowed off the roads so the going was pretty good.

"A doe came down from a steep sidehill and crossed the

road about 100 yards ahead of them heading towards the river. They parked the Jeep and watched, expecting a buck to be following. Instead, less than a minute later, a big cougar bounded across the road. It was after the deer and paid the Jeep no attention. The river was only a couple of hundred feet down below. The cougar scrambled across the rocks to the other side and went up into the timber. The deer went upstream a bit, then stood in the water up to its belly.

"At that time we were living at Abbotsford in the Fraser Valley. One hunter stayed to watch while the other drove back to Hope and phoned me to bring the hounds and get up there as soon as possible. When I got there at about 10:30 the deer was still standing in the river.

"It took another half hour to get across the river and walk up the other side. One hunter came with me while the other guarded the deer. We were opposite the Jeep and up from the river a bit when we hit the cougar's tracks. We hadn't gone 50 yards until I noticed a lynx track on top of the cougar trail. Another 50 yards ahead I saw the cougar walking along a log. When I shouted he just leisurely put his big paws up on a tree, climbed to the first limb and sat there. I put a bullet behind his front shoulder and let the hounds go. Twenty yards further we came onto a half-eaten lynx that was still warm, then walked on up to get the cougar. When we dragged the big tom back down to where he had eaten breakfast we stopped a while.

"Reading the story by the signs in the snow, I could easily see where the lynx had been attracted by the twitching of the cougar's tail as it lay watching the deer. When the lynx sprang at this movement the bigger cat smashed its skull with a deadly blow.

"All this had happened so silently that the hunter across the river, not 200 yards away had not heard a sound. When we dragged the cougar on down to the river the little doe ran

179

out and scrambled up the bank into the timber. This was the first and only time I actually found where a cougar had killed and eaten a lynx," Jack concluded.

"Weren't you called to Lytton in the early seventies? There was a fatal attack on a 12-year-old boy there in January of 1971. It was across the bridge where the Thompson River joins the Fraser."

"Yes, we were just starting lunch when the phone rang. The Lytton police wanted me up there as fast as possible. That would mean 70 miles of snow and ice to drive through from Abbotsford. In January the days are short. It's getting dark by four in the afternoon. I was rushing to get there while it was still light enough to shoot. Near Boston Bar with some 25 miles still to go the Lytton police got me by radio phone. They told me the cougar and boy were both dead. I went with the police to help bring in the cougar and see what had happened.

"Three children, a boy of 12 and his younger sisters, ages six and eight, had been sliding on the snow near the railway tracks about a quarter of a mile from their home. They were sliding down into a gulley where two big culverts went under the railway. One of the culverts was at the bottom and the other was up the side about 15 feet higher. The children apparently got tired of sliding and ran through the higher culvert to go under the tracks. The boy came out of the other end first. The cougar smashed his skull and began dragging him off into some trees. The two little girls screamed, went back through the culvert and ran home to tell their parents. They said a bobcat had got Larry and was dragging him away. Mr. Wells took nothing more than his hunting knife to the gully. He figured he could take care of a bobcat with that. Their mother found the rifle and some shells and followed. Her little daughters showed her where to go.

"When they got there the dad was looking into the wrong

place. He came up and took the rifle and then went through the top culvert. He came out on the other side to see the big cougar licking the blood and chewing at his son's head. He didn't know whether or not his boy was alive so he fired a shot to try to scare the animal away. It just growled and began dragging the boy further into the trees.

"This movement separated the two far enough apart so that it was safe to try another shot. Wells hit the cougar in the guts. It let go of the boy and staggered off up the hill. The man picked up his son and carried him to their house. Half the boy's head was missing. A terrible thing for the little girls to see. We found the cougar dead some distance further up the trail.

"When I investigated the scene the next morning, the tracks showed where the killer had walked around their house several times the night before, then bedded down to watch the trail. He had slept only a short distance from the Wells' home. The tracks clearly showed where the cougar had followed the children as they went out to play.

"When I skinned the animal and cut open the stomach it contained only some blood and other parts of the boy's head. He was a large adult male, not carrying much fat. This animal showed no fear of humans. This was evident by the places he had gone when I backtracked the day after. That cougar was looking for food when he took the boy."

Jack told of another attack in the Pitt Lake area a few years later.

"In June 1975 I was called to Pitt Lake to take care of a cougar that had attacked a boy. It's only about an hour's drive from our home in Abbotsford to get to where it happened. I crossed the Pitt River Bridge on Highway 7 and turned up the road towards the lake. The boy's father took me and the hounds by boat the last mile. He showed me where the cougar went into the woods. I turned the dogs loose and the would-be killer was up a tree and shot in less than half an hour. We dragged it out then proceeded to take out the guts and examine the critter. She was between two and three years old and had better than half a raccoon in her stomach. It was by far the fattest cougar I had ever shot. There was over two inches of fat to cut through before we could clean her out. The boy's dad then proceeded to explain what had happened.

"To protect the people involved, no names should be mentioned here. The father with his children had pulled their boat up on a sand bar. The two youngsters ran up the beach to the edge of the woods. The boy was a few yards ahead. The cougar jumped out and knocked him down then started dragging him off. His sister ran back to tell her father. Snatching an oar out of the boat he ran the 100 yards and beat the cougar until she dropped the boy and disappeared. He picked up his unconscious son, carried him to the boat, then rowed across the river to call an ambulance.

"The young lad was taken to the nearest hospital, examined and released the next day. Tho' there were teeth marks on the back of the boy's neck, no one considered his condition serious. However, several months later, he began having pains in his neck and head. An X-ray showed two fractured vertebrae.

"Actually, he was lucky to come out of it alive. Had he been turned or moved the wrong way while his dad was carrying him, he could have died on the spot.

"A couple of years later I met his father at Abbotsford. He told me his son had not been right since the time he was bitten."

"That's about the worst I've heard, Jack, but maybe there are others," I said.

"Plenty more. Just over a year later, in August 1976, the Coquitlam (a Vancouver suburb) police called to say there were some problem cougar near the edge of town. I put four hounds in the pickup and went down early next morning. There was an old female with three grown kittens prowling about and terrorizing the neighbourhood. One of the big cats had chased a woman into her house three times in one day. When she threw a shoe at it the cougar ripped the top to shreds and then walked off with the remains. That was when she called the police.

"Several people had lost dogs and now the cougar were taking their chickens. The police had waited on top of a chicken house the night before until the old female came for another chicken, then killed her with buckshot.

"When I put the hounds out, the first thing they treed was a wounded 70-pound tom. I shot it and found a pellet lodged in its nose. It took me another day to get the two remaining cats. I sure as hell wasn't going away, leaving wounded cougar in the bush.

"That's just a few instances. I've been called out to shoot several hundred predators since joining the game department," Jack concluded.

Dan and I had been listening to his dad with great interest and I asked, "Dan, how about bringing us up-to-date with some of your experiences."

"Well, I didn't really get started on Vancouver Island until 1973. Reading some reports from the years before it looked like a busy time ahead. Skate Hames had reported a hunter being attacked by a young cougar between Courtenay and Cumberland. In June 1972 Al Hurford was mauled in his sleeping bag while camping near Campbell Lake. Then, in July, the same year, eight-year-old Bob Kelly was mauled at Miller Creek near Campbell River.

"I'd hardly got settled before calls started coming in. There were half a dozen in the first month. I had to shoot one bear and several cougar before we got properly moved in.

183

"The incident that impressed me most was in late April of 1974. Port Alberni police called the game department about a cougar inside city limits. I loaded our cage, put in the hounds and headed out. The dogs treed the cat in short order.

"I tranquillized the young tom and took it to Northwest Bay. Percy Dewar and his wife were doing a cougar study for the department. They were putting on beeper collars, then keeping records of what the collared animals did. Before leaving, I asked them to let me know immediately should they loose track of this particular cat.

"'He could be dangerous,' I warned them. About two weeks later, a call came in from Cowichan Lake. Some sheep had been killed. The farmer the previous day had called in neighbour who kept hounds. With no luck. By the time my hounds got there, the trail was 18 hours old. The farmer thought I was too late to be able to follow the trail but he did show me where his sheep had been killed. There was an old railway grade that went through a swamp just outside his pasture fence.

"'No use going in that swamp. The other dogs were in there yesterday,' he told me.

"Telling him I would have a look anyway I climbed the fence and walked along the old grade. About half a mile further there was a bit of wool stuck to some brush. Pretty soon my two hounds started to get excited, then gave tongue on a fresh trail. The cougar ran for about a half mile before it climbed a fir tree. I took a good look with my binoculars and saw the cat was collared.

"Leaving the dogs I rushed back to the pickup then called my boss for permission to shoot the killer. I told him I was positive it was the same cougar that was taken to the Dewars from Alberni. There was a long silence. Shooting a collared cougar without good reason was a 'no no.'

"'If you are sure it's the same cat, go ahead and shoot it," he agreed.

"Letting the two young hounds out of their cage we ran back to the tree. A bullet behind the ear did the job. The number on the collar proved it to be the one the Dewars had tagged and released only two weeks earlier. That was fifty miles north of where the sheep had been killed. I took the collar back to the Dewars that same afternoon. They didn't explain why they hadn't let me know about the cougar leaving their study area. Might have saved the farmer some sheep."

He went on to tell of a fairly recent killing of a seven-year-old Indian girl only a few miles out of the town of Gold River. This mill town is almost in the centre of Vancouver Island out on the West Coast.

In mid July 1976, the *Victoria Colonist* reported the killing and Dan handed me the clipping, stating, "This is a good report and probably better than I can remember the tragic event," and it read:

The results of an autopsy on a cougar which killed a seven-year-old Port Alberni girl in an unprovoked attack near Gold River Wednesday are expected to be known later today.

The male animal, which measured eight feet from nose to tail tip, pounced on Matilda May Samuel while she was berry picking along a gravel road with Jack Richard Johnson, 17, and Jeffie Joseph, 15, both of the nearby Mowachah Indian reserve. The victim had been visiting an aunt on the reserve and was to have returned to her home today.

One person keenly awaiting the outcome of the autopsy is fish and wildlife branch predator hunter Dan Lay of Nanaimo, who shot the animal several hours later and about 200 yards from the fatal attack site.

"Something had gone haywire," said Lay, whose experience as the predator hunter has shown him that cougars usually give humans a wide berth. He further described the killer cougar as a "peculiar cat" in the way it circled back when Lay and his four hounds were in pursuit.

"With the amount of people and noise coming from the road, it should have run off," he said. Lay shot the animal with two .30-.30 bullets to the head after the animal fled fifty feet up a tree.

Also indicating the animal was "not a typical cougar," according to Lay, was a report of what is believed to have been the same animal earlier chasing a motorcyclist along the road in the area of the fatal attack.

Lay said all unusual behavior in cougars, which generally means either aggression or no fear of humans, should be reported. Authorities only learned of the motorcyclist's experience after the attack on the girl. Lay cautioned hikers, campers and anyone else to avoid wild animals "like the plague."

"You've got to respect these animals; they are not something you can walk up to talk to, even though television and movies seem to say you can," Lay said.

Anyone meeting a cougar face-to-face, according to Lay, should stand upright and shout and wave their arms while backing up slowly.

"Nine out of ten times it will turn and run," Lay said. But people shouldn't turn and run which will only make the cat curious and likely to give pursuit.

"In the rare instance that a cougar stalks or gives chase," Lay said, "fleeing up a tree is the best defence. It allows a person to fend off the cat with their foot and gives the animal less body surface to attack."

Lay estimated he has killed 10 cougars since the start of the year with the only Greater Victoria region kill coming in several months ago in the Rocky Point area where a cougar was bothering sheep.

But Lay said the number is not unusually high. In 1974, he had six killings in one month.

However, on the Lower Mainland, Lay's father Jack, a predator control officer for the last 21 years, said he has never had so many reports of cougar sightings as in the last two years.

A provincial conservation officer shot a cougar in North Vancouver Wednesday after it was treed by three dogs which were on a walk with a woman. The cougar was first sighted in the area July 1 but had eluded hunting attempts.

One North Vancouver family reported that the cougar had tried to attack the family dog through a sliding glass door from an outside patio.

The autopsy showed the cougar to be fat and in good condition. It was almost three years old, a male with food in its stomach. There was also a quantity of the girl's blood.

"That just goes to show how important it is for everyone to report any and all cougar sightings. Especially those near towns," Dan emphasized, although admitting this was not always possible.

Jack Lay went on to explain. "Supposing a farmer sees a cougar killing a sheep or packing his dog away about six a.m. on a Saturday. He can't call the game department because those offices are closed until Monday. By that time, it is likely to be too late to do anything about it anyway. If there was a number to call and leave a message on a recording device, it wouldn't be much trouble or cost to have this checked at least once every day on weekends and holidays. It could save a lot of trouble for very little money," he figured.

Jack illustrated how unpredictable a cougar really is, saying, "There is no set pattern for how often or how many deer or sheep or what quantity or part of the animal they will eat. I was called out to a little five-acre farm where the farmer only had five sheep. He put them in his barn every night to protect them from dogs and coyotes.

"The morning he called me, he had gone out to find all five dead. They were laying out on the plank floor with their throats torn out. The floor was swept every day so it was clean. That cougar, a big tom, had drunk all the blood. There wasn't a sign on the floor anywhere. He had licked up every drop. I shot him when he came back for a feed that evening. This was right near town and less than 100 feet from the back door of the farmer's house.

"Another time I was called up to Williams Lake in February. There was about two feet of snow. The weather was bitter cold. A lot of mule deer winter in this area. A cattle rancher had seen the cougar prowling about and called the game

187

warden. When I got there we went to have a look. He had killed seven deer and taken nothing but the blood. Seems to be what most adult males do before they take off on the prowl, looking for females.

"I tracked that old devil for six days. He was into every log pile and cougar den for 60 miles. He neither killed nor ate a single bit of food in all that time. Neither did he find a female. On the seventh day I caught up with him. He had found a female. That was his end."

"How does a full-grown cougar usually stalk and kill a deer?" I asked.

"There is no set pattern. In the Interior where the country is more open they usually try to spot a feeding deer. They watch for a while to find out the direction the deer is moving, then take a circle and sneak up to a place the deer may pass. Here they lay and wait. If there is snow, usually there will be a fan-shaped mark where the end of the tail twitches back and forth.

"When a deer comes close enough, the cougar will spring and pull it over with claws hooked onto the nose. If it's a doe or a buck without horns, one bite between the ears with those big fangs is enough to kill any deer instantly. If it's a full-grown buck with antlers the killer will usually bite into the underside of the neck. By reading the signs when there is snow it looks like a cougar can 'bulldog' a deer or an elk about as fast and as easily as a good cowboy does a steer in a rodeo contest.

"A young deer or fawn is usually stunned with a smack by a front paw. The cougar will then tear open the rib cage, eat the heart and liver, then drink the blood from the opening in the chest cavity. From the bigger animals, the blood is most often taken from the throat.

"All of these ways of killing are nothing more than the

usual run of things. A cougar seems to do anything that comes into its head at any given time.

"I was tracking a grown cat in about six inches of new snow a few years ago. He was travelling in steep country. It was easy to tell he was hunting. While angling up a mountain some 3,000 feet over a course of about four miles he had laid to watch at several vantage points. Then, for no apparent reason, he took off down the mountainside doing jumps of 30 feet or more. He went clear to the bottom then turned around and walked straight back up again."

"Why would he do that?" I asked.

"He was trying to flush out a deer. At the speed he would be travelling, nothing could outrun him to get away. Some hours later he did the same thing further along. This time he flushed a deer out of a thicket. The young buck didn't run a 100 feet until it was bowled over and killed.

"In those days we shot any cougar that was molesting game. That was our job. I've hunted and trapped for over 35 years and have come to the conclusion that cougar are opportunists. If someone tells you an animal will do this or that at any given time, it's not so. No two cougar are alike. Some will swim a lake or river for no apparent reason while others can't be chased into the water. They all drink blood but some far more than others. I don't believe any of them know what they are going to do next until it happens. They are unpredictable and dangerous."

I asked Dan what he thought of the wolf population on Vancouver Island.

"Well, the deer population north of Campbell River is only about a quarter of what it was a few years ago. The wolves have eaten about everything that walks, swims or crawls in that part of the country. They are now feeding from garbage dumps or anywhere food is discarded.

"I caught one in a trap last winter at Nanaimo River wearing a beeper collar that was put on at Kelsey Bay. That's over 100 miles south from where it was tagged. Wolves don't usually travel that far unless they are hungry.

"As you know, Joe, there is a fair number of deer in the Nanaimo River area. The wolves are thinning them out in spite of our trapping program. I believe the wolves are forcing the cougar toward the east and into the farming and more-settled areas. Reports of sightings and stock killing are definitely on the increase all along the east side of Vancouver Island.

"If it's not the wolves then it's the mature tom cougar that are forcing the two- and three-year-old males out of the woods into civilization. Over 50 per cent of the cougar I take from settled areas have been scarred up from fighting.

"A few months ago we tranquilized a young three-year-old tom near Port Alberni. We were doing a deer study using beeper collars in the Nanaimo Lakes District so we decided to put a collar on this cat and release him out there so we could keep track of what he did and where he went. He stayed around for a couple of weeks and then we didn't hear him any more.

"About a week later, one of our vehicles was out doing a routine check to the west of Cowichan Lake. It picked up his signal but it was on the signal that only comes on if the animal is dead! When we followed the fast beeps, the cougar was found in a draw not too far from an old logging road.

"There was no sign of a fight. The only marks on his body were two big fang holes in the back of his head. When I skinned out the skull for a better look, the fangs had gone through the bone and into the brain.

"The cougar that did the killing proceeded to leave plenty of scratch mounds to show his territory boundary. We couldn't be sure but it looked as if the younger cougar had

190

just crouched down expecting friendship. Instead, he got the kiss of death!

"I found only one other young tom that was killed for trespassing on a bigger cougar's range. There had been a terrible fight. The dead animal had been ripped, clawed and bitten in the head."

"Have you ever come on a pair of mating cougar?" I asked.

"No, but I tracked a pair in the snow for the best part of two days in February of 1978. They just wandered about from one patch of timber to the next. There was a young tom that followed along keeping some hours behind.

"This smaller male seemed frustrated. He was making 'scratches,' small amounts of dirt or other material scratched up to form mounds and then thoroughly saturated with urine to mark territory boundaries, about every 200 yards or so. He would wander away from the trail of the mating pair then bound back to leave more scratches. This female was shot by a hunter. When I finally caught up she was in the back of a pickup truck. Apart from being scuffed up a bit she just plain stunk.

"In the fall of 1982 there was a call from our conservation office in Port Hardy. A cougar had been seen on the military base at Holberg. This town is almost at the northern tip of Vancouver Island right out on the West Coast. The prowler had knocked a child down and chased a house cat right up onto a back porch. When I called the commanding officer of the base he didn't think it necessary to have the animal taken away. I warned him of the potential danger and suggested he mail a letter to our Port Hardy office stating his position.

"Two days later a call came in asking me to get up there in a hurry. Apparently this same cougar had threatened a man in the parking area the following day. When I arrived next evening there was a crowd of people just inside the gates at the base. A young boy on his bicycle had been chased down

191

the road and knocked over when the cougar pounced on him. The young lad had got up and was attempting to fend off the snarling animal with his bike. Just then a car came down the road and probably saved the boy's life. The big cat backed off and jumped into the thick brush.

"I got there a few minutes later with six hounds. I let them all go. They put the cougar up a tree after a wild chase. It was dark by the time we dragged the dead animal out to the road. It was not the type of cougar to be tranquilized and moved to another location.

"There had been more than 650 cases recorded where cougar had molested people or killed pets and livestock by the time I left the department," Jack said.

There also had been 16,287 government bounties paid from 1910 until the bounty was discontinued at the end of 1956. Bounties ranged from $10 to $40. The bounty total is taken from a report printed by the Fish and Wildlife Branch.

The three of us had spent a most interesting and informative afternoon and as we said good-bye, Jack smiled, "Sorry to rush away like this but the wife and I have a date up island to catch some salmon come daylight tomorrow."

Bush Flying

In 1949 I learned float flying on Quamichan Lake near Duncan. My pilot's licence number P1799 was approved June 19, 1950. Brother Tom already had licence P1396. He had become interested a couple of years earlier and took his instruction at Cassidy Airport, south of Nanaimo. Just days after getting his licence, he went to the United States, bought and flew back the first Seabee ever registered in B.C.

This little four-place flying boat with its retractable wheels could land on either water or runway. Its motor was mounted behind the wings so it was called a pusher. The propeller was supposed to change pitch or go into reverse when a knob was pulled on the instrument panel. We soon learned in cold weather that this change in pitch didn't always happen. With all the lakes, rivers and saltchuck on the coast to land on, it certainly was much more practical and safer than a wheel aircraft. By June 1949 Tom had traded in his Seabee on a Cessna 195 on floats.

"What's wrong with the Seabee?" I asked, when he told me what he had paid extra for the new Cessna.

"Nothing really wrong. The only thing I don't like about it is that it doesn't glide much better than a brick if the engine quits."

Tom had a first class big game guiding licence. Because he used his aircraft to commute between hunting camps and civilization he volunteered to act as a flying game warden.

Frank Butler, then in charge of the game department, welcomed Tom's offer. I was covering other areas in my own plane and Butler asked me to report on game infractions on these flights.

Float planes got us into the remote areas in a matter of minutes rather than days and sometimes weeks of tough slogging to reach these by pack horses or on foot.

One evening we were flying up the Chilco River to stay the night at Chilco Lake Lodge. We had seen several small bands of wild horses along the ridges south of the river. About 10 minutes from the lodge, at 5,000 feet we were only about 800 feet above the terrain. We rounded a turn in the river and, standing on an open ridge, was a beautiful snow-white stallion, head high, his main and tail blowing in the wind. I watched him rear to stand on his hind legs and paw the air. His mouth was open. I'm sure he was screaming a warning to his harem of mares.

"I'll circle for a better look," Tom said as he banked the plane.

We counted more than 50 horses grazing within half a mile of the stallion. We flew over him again and he reared then trotted from his lofty lookout. The last we saw of him he was galloping about, forcing the mares up toward the timber. Several times that summer we again spotted his band of horses. By the next year many of them had disappeared. Cowboys and Indian bands were rounding them up and selling them.

194

In June of 1949 the ice was almost gone on most of the higher lakes in the Chilcotin. Tom and I were flying in to see how our hunting cabins had come through the winter. Circling low over Schalligan Lake before landing we spotted five moose lying in the willows near the water's edge. We checked the cabin, then taxied the plane to where we had seen the moose. Three were already dead. The last two were yearlings and barely alive. Although they could raise up on their front legs the back half of their bodies were completely paralyzed. Along the backs of all these moose we counted over two dozen gray-black ticks. These parasites were about the size of the end of a man's index finger to the first joint.

The animals had struggled and slowly died of starvation. We decided to put the two dying ones out of their misery. We had a 30-30 carbine in the plane. This was one of the times it was put to good use.

It appeared to us that the paralysis came on from the hind quarters and slowly progressed forward. Some of the dead animals had dragged themselves through the mud for a half-mile. They had eaten every twig and branch they could reach, down to about three quarters of an inch in diameter.

We landed on Tesunia Lake near Jack Blatsford's ranch. He told us he had seen more than 30 dead moose while tending his cattle.

"All have those big ticks in their backs. I shot six that were unable to get on their feet."

"We'll report this to the game department," Tom promised.

"Think that will do any good?" Blatsford asked sceptically.

"Makes you realize just how cruel nature can be when you see what really goes on," Tom said grimly, as we took off for Toutrie Lake.

We saw several more dead moose. At the end of the lake two more were struggling among the willows. We turned back and landed. I took the rifle and waded ashore. Getting up close to those two half-dead creatures was an unforgettable experience. Their eyes showed great agony as they lay their heads on the mud facing me. There was not the slightest sign of a struggle when a bullet ended their suffering. On the back of the young cow I counted 27 big ticks.

"Maybe we should drop in at Meldrum Creek and see Eric Collier," Tom suggested.

"Sure, why not. It's only about 15 miles out of our way."

Eric was a game guide and a keen conservationist. He had been battling with the game department, through the B.C. Guides Association, to stop the shooting of cow moose for the past five years. When we taxied up to the shore of his beaver pond he was waiting.

After a handshake, his first words were, "Moose around here are dying like flies. Ticks have just about cleaned them out. I've shot over a dozen paralyzed animals along my trapline this spring."

"Have you reported this to Frank Butler?" asked Tom.

"Frank was here only last week. He's assigned a young biologist named Jim Hatter to do a study and see what can be done. By the time the study is half finished, the tick cycle will be gone and so will most of our moose," Collier figured, his voice showing disgust.

"We've just come in from Chilco Lake. There are dead or dying moose from here to there," I told him.

We walked up to his cabin and had some tea while Eric showed us dozens of letters he had written to the B.C. Game Department.

"This tick problem should certainly be high on the agenda of our guides' meeting next month," Tom insisted.

Eric told us Butler had apologized for not closing the cow moose season. With some protection and a reduced bag limit, it is amazing how fast the moose population recovered.

During 1954 I did a lot of cruising up along the Fraser

River. Here, on Sheep Creek Hill, the game department had built a huge corral to capture some of the California bighorn sheep that stayed on the steep ridges above the river. I watched as they tried for months to drive the wild sheep into this man-made enclosure.

They were breaking camp, ready to give up. The night before they were leaving the cook threw some cabbage that was spoiling out into the corral. Next morning, there were over 30 sheep inside, chomping on the cabbage. The biologist closed the gate, then selected and loaded the 20 animals they wanted for relocating in Oregon into a semi-trailer cattle truck.

About six miles south of the corral, 12 other big rams stood on a ridge, watched the plane go by as I flew out.

The 20 sheep sent to Oregon have multiplied and are doing well after 30 years. They are now the base stock for several other new bands in the U.S.A.

On September 5, 1958 Tom was killed when his Cessna 180 crashed in Desolation Sound just east of Redonda Island. The water was flat, glassy and apparently his altimeter was over-reading. His floats hit before he was in a landing attitude. The impact was so great it buckled both floats and killed Tom and his passenger instantly. This was a terrible shock to our family.

Just a year after Tom's death a close friend of mine was killed in the same area. Larry Lyttle and myself were the only two pilots on the coast who had flown Piper Pacers on floats for any great length of time. We usually got together at least once every two months to compare notes and discuss experiences.

The last time we talked we both agreed our planes would certainly handle a lot better if they were not so short-coupled and cranky on the water. Larry said he almost nosed in and damaged his propeller a few days before. I had recently dipped a wingtip in some rough water and a strong side wind had almost flipped her over.

"Maybe we should trade them in on a 180 or something like that," were his last words as we parted.

Less than a week later he got caught in a down draft and struck a guyline of a spar tree situated just above his logging camp on the northeast of East Redonda Island. Larry and his two passengers were killed and the plane was a total wreck, scattered over a mile of the rough hillside.

This morning while reminiscing through my pilot's logbook, I notice the last flight recorded is dated September 22, 1960. This trip was from Redonda to Campbell River and then down to Quamichan Lake near Duncan.

After 24 years the memories are very clear; some surprising and some sad. There is still a strong yearning to look down on the islands from a low altitude and see the deer, cougar and other wildlife in their natural habitat.

I feel sure that our initial plans for helicopter logging will one day become substantially successful. We were 20 years too soon because the choppers of the 1960's didn't have enough lifting capacity.

I miss my friends that have gone on before me. I miss the flying, the hunting trips and just tramping around the woods.

But I'm still lucky, at 75, to be able to fire up the old four-wheel drive and cruise some of the outback logging roads. We watch the deer and shoot the odd grouse. It's always pleasant to study and marvel at nature. For a change of pace it's fun to tease Ruby when she can't tell the difference between a hemlock and a fir tree.

Epilogue

Frank Greenfield, November 1978
Born February 17, 1902 at Shathroy, Ontario. Died November 22, 1984
at Nanaimo, British Columbia.

He was one of the last two remaining officers of those who
started the Fish and Wildlife Branch in 1929.

Up to 1955, he held the record for catching the most
poachers and pitlampers throughout British Columbia.

During the hungry thirties, it was not unusual for some
needy family to hear a heavy thump on the porch after dark.

When they went to investigate, there would be meat and groceries in a box or bag. By the time the door opened, Frank made sure he was out of sight.

Herbert Greenfield, Frank's father, was born in Winchester, England November 26, 1865. He came to Canada in 1892 to settle in Strathroy, Ontario.

It was here he courted and married Elizabeth Harris in 1900. Their two sons were born here.

In the spring of 1906 this young family packed their belongings and moved to Alberta. They travelled north of Edmonton some 50 miles and started a homestead near the settlement of Westlock.

Herbert was a successful farmer and was a driving force in organizing the United Farmers of Alberta. Known as the U.F.A., this group became a very powerful political party. Mr. Greenfield was Vice-President when the U.F.A. party soundly defeated the Liberals in the general provincial election in August of 1921. He was nominated and elected leader of the party that same month.

At this time, Greenfield did not have a seat in the legislature. In a by-election he was elected for Peace River district December 9, 1921. Mr. Greenfield now became Premier of Alberta.

He also shouldered the load of two other important portfolios, Provincial Secretary and Provincial Treasurer.

He shaped the government to his liking and wasted no time in bringing in legislation that would help the farmers and other workers.

The Alberta Wheat Pool was established in 1923 and became a powerful selling agent for the farmers.

Prohibition was abolished and the sale of liquor taken over by the government.

He appointed the first Minimum Wage Board in Alberta.

The Workmen's Compensation Act was amended to make it fair for all.

1923 also saw the birth of the Debt Adjustment Act, designed to help the debt-laden farmers.

These accomplishments made the people of the province very satisfied with their new government and its premier.

Because of criticism from a radical group in the party, Mr. Greenfield resigned as Premier November 23, 1925.

He was appointed the Agent General for Alberta and was in London, England from 1927-31.

After his return to Alberta he was associated with the petroleum industry.

Franklin Harris Greenfield was the eldest of their two sons. In the fall of 1924, he met Marian Cuming when she came out from Edmonton to visit friends at Westlock. There followed a whirlwind courtship. Min (as she is known to all her friends) was seventeen and Frank was twenty-two. They were married in Edmonton on February 17, 1925. Min was Frank's 23rd birthday present. They had over 59 good years together.

They moved out to Victoria in the fall of 1926. Frank worked in the Eaton's department store for a few months. This kind of work he hated. He wanted to be outdoors.

The next spring he got a job at the Government Pheasant Farm in Saanich some fifteen miles north of Victoria. He bought a Model-T Ford and managed to commute daily. The job was 10 hours, 6 days a week.

In Frank's own words, "I loved every minute of it."

The game farm consisted of about 150 acres with 10 acres fenced. They raised some 4,000 pheasants each year. These were released all over Vancouver Island and the Lower Mainland. Frank, by now, had joined the Provincial Police and was in charge of distribution of the birds.

In September of 1929, he was given the choice of being

posted to Cowichan Lake or Nanaimo as game warden. He chose Nanaimo. Next Monday morning he was in charge of the large central Vancouver Island district.

Frank rented a house on the corner of Comox Road and Fraser Street right where the Texaco gas station now stands. Being in a hurry he hadn't investigated the area. Fraser Street, at that time, was a flourishing red light district. Most of the traffic in or out of the houses had to pass by their door.

Min and her baby daughter had hardly got nicely settled, when one of "the ladies of the night" from across the street paid them a visit. This young lady had knitted a beautiful pink sweater for the baby and presented it as a gift.

When Mrs. Greenfield learned what this young lady did for a living she was most upset. Her daughter told me she was never allowed to wear that sweater.

It is needless to say Frank lost little time in moving the family to a different part of town.

He soon became well known in the district and was respected because he prosecuted poachers when caught but if the man was in need of meat, during the thirties, he would keep out of sight and let the needy ones pack their deer home unmolested.

Pitlamping was a criminal offence. Many a rainy night Frank spent out in the woods when he knew lamping was being done. He told me how he had met Jim Dewar for the first time in the early thirties.

"I was out back near the Waterworks Dam above the Nanaimo River looking for pitlampers when I saw a light coming toward me down the narrow road. I hid in the bush and waited. When the light was opposite me, I jumped out and stopped the man, shouting, 'Police! Halt and stand where you are.' Jim stopped and his two big cougar hounds came up and stood beside him. He had no gun and his carbide miner's lamp barely gave enough light for him to recognize me.

"Jim, with a big grin, stuck out his hand and in that quiet voice remarked, 'Why hello Frank! Sure didn't expect to see you this far back so late at night. I'm Jim Dewar and this is Patsy and Blue, my new hounds. You looking for somebody?' he asked.

"'Got word of some night hunters and came out to investigate,' I said.

"'Sorry I can't stick around to help. I have to get on through to Youbou for the morning shift at the sawmill,' Jim explained.

"'How many miles from here?' I asked.

"'About eighteen miles from where I get on that bush trail at the end of this road. Hope to see you again soon.' He walked away into the darkness. That was the start of the finest friendship any man could ever hope for. For the rest of Jim's life we were as close or maybe even closer than brothers."

That's how Greenfield summed up their association.

I visited John Mihalech shortly after Christmas of 1984. John used to own and operate the Chase River Market on the highway just south of Nanaimo.

After the mines closed he worked in the woods. He was a good rigging man and could handle loading or yarding machines. John always was a keen hunter and fisherman. That's how his family got enough to eat during the depression years.

John told me about an unusual series of events that happened during the last weekend of September in 1935.

"Four of us drove out to our cabin from Extension in my 1928 Chevrolet touring car. We left Friday evening after a shift in the coal mine. We were only working two or three days a week and needed some venison to feed our families. I only saw one good buck and missed it. That was Sunday afternoon.

"It was pouring rain and getting dark when I got back to the cabin. After some rye bread and beans I decided to fire up my carbide lamp and go after the buck I had missed. I figured no self-respecting game warden would stay out in this kind of weather.

"I shot my buck, a nice two pointer, cleaned it out and dragged it up near the trail then hid it under a bushy tree.

"I was almost back to our cabin when suddenly a flashlight shone in my face. Frank Greenfield stepped out of the bush, took my gun and lamp then snapped a pair of handcuffs on my wrists.

"'I'm putting you in jail,' he announced.

"It was just past eleven o'clock when Frank left me in the jail at Nanaimo with Officer Gunn. I was allowed to phone Gunn's superior, Mr. Russel. He agreed to let me go home to put on some dry clothes and be back before 9:00 a.m. to stand trial in the morning.

"Instead of going home, I persuaded my brother Mike to drive me back to the scene of the crime. I wanted to tell my buddies I was in jail so they wouldn't start a search. We were also intending to bring in the deer and hang it up for proper cooling.

"We were almost there when the flashlight shone in our faces.

"'Hey, I just put you in jail!' Frank blurted out in disbelief.

"When I explained what had happened, Frank escorted me to the cabin then promptly took me back to jail.

"At nine-thirty sharp next morning, I was up before Magistrate Beevor-Potts. He sentenced me to 30 days in Okalla or a 500 dollar fine.

"Mr. Greenfield quickly reminded the magistrate that the laws had recently been changed and that the minimum was 60 days or $500. I didn't have the money so we were on the afternoon boat for Okalla Prison in New Westminster. Most loggers called it 'The Crowbar Hotel'.

"The second week there came a letter from home. The family had no wood, no food and no prospect of things improving. I borrowed some writing paper and wrote to Mr. Sloan, the Attorney-General. I explained how it would be much cheaper for the province if they let me go home and look after my family. The wife's letter was attached to mine.

"On the 28th day of my sentence I was allowed to go home on probation.

"The cash allowance for a prisoner was 10¢ per day. My fare on the boat was paid by the government so I had over $2.00 cash in my pocket when I got home to Extension."

"Did you ever pitlamp again?" I asked.

"Never! I was cured," John said with a grin.

"Well your little episode puts both you and Greenfield in an unusual position. You are the only man in the province to be jailed twice in one night for pitlamping and Frank is the only Conservation Officer to catch the same man twice in a single night."

John gave me a copy of the *Daily Colonist* dated Friday, January 13, 1967 that tells about this event. It goes on to praise Mr. Greenfield for his interesting and dedicated career as a "Game Warden."

The article explains that during his last 30 years, Frank worked with Mr. C. Mottley on extensive rainbow trout studies. He also worked with Biologist Don Robinson on the first blacktail deer studies on Vancouver Island.

Frank, after 40 years with the Game Department retired at the end of February 1967. He was a member of the Nanaimo Fish and Game Club from 1929 on.

To me, he was one of the greatest and most dedicated conservationists this province has ever known.

Let this epilogue be a challenge to all members of our Fish

2630 Departure Bay Rd
Nanaimo, B.C. V9S-3W5

Mr Joe Garner :—
Nanaimo, B.C.

Dear Joe :—

I have just read your new book, Never
a time to trust. Congratulations, You made
a wonderful job of it.

Yours also was a fitting tribute to
the memory of the late Jim Dewar, as a
woodsman & a hunter, Jim knew no peer,
he was the best.

I also note some criticism of certain
methods & policies of Government & the Fish
& Wild Life Branch. Your criticism is well
founded & I hope that the powers that
be will take notice of it.

Thank you for the book. I have enjoyed
reading it & I can assure you that it
will be read many, many more times.

Sincerely
Frank Greenfield

and Game Clubs—to our Local and Regional Politicians and to the Provincial Government to establish a visible lasting heritage honouring our unsung wilderness heroes.

How about starting with such men as Bryan Williams, Frank Butler, Jim Dewar and Frank Greenfield?

Let us have a Hall of Fame, a Wall of Fame, a Portrait or a Bronze Plaque in some appropriate location.

The letter on the left is not dated. It was postmarked November 22, 1984.

Frank's eldest daughter explained, "Dad wrote the letter in the morning. He and mother went to Woodgrove, just north of Nanaimo, to mail the letter and do some shopping. He was feeling poorly and just wanted to sit on a bench when he got the chance. On the way home on the bus he was having trouble breathing and tried to open a window for some fresh air.

"The bus driver parked the bus to help Mother and Dad across the street to their walkway. Dad only went about another thirty feet when he slumped backwards. An ambulance came to take him to the hospital. He was pronounced dead on arrival."